50 PEOPLE WHO BUGGERED UP BRITAIN

50 PEOPLE WHO BUGGERED UP BRITAIN

QUENTIN LETTS

Constable • London

Constable and Robinson
3 The Lanchesters
162 Fulham Palace Road
London W6 9ER
www.constablerobinson.com

Published in the UK by Constable,
an imprint of Constable & Robinson Ltd 2008

A copy of the British Library cataloguing in Publication Data is
available from the British Library.

ISBN 978-1-84529-855-5

Printed and bound in the EU

1 3 5 7 9 10 8 6 4 2

Mixed Sources
Product group from well-managed
forests and other controlled sources
www.fsc.org Cert no. SA-COC-1565
© 1996 Forest Stewardship Council
FSC

Dedicated to my darling wife Lois,
who puts up with me shouting at the television

Contents

Acknowledgements

Thanks to the following for their help and advice: Andreas Campomar, the *Daily Mail* library and its staff, Sir Andrew Green, Nicola Jennings, Anthony Kilmister, Hilary Lowinger, Maggie Pearlstine, Sue Roccelli and Gill Watmough.

Introduction

Shrivelled old Enoch, bony forefinger describing the horizon, said forty years ago in his papery voice that he saw 'a nation busily engaged in building its own funeral pyre'. Moulded by his colour-prejudiced era, Powell supposed that 'the black man' would have 'the whip hand' by the year 1988.

Well, it has taken a little longer than that and has proved a great deal more complicated. Colour grievance has been but one blight on British life. 'The black man' has turned out to be just as likely a bossy white woman wielding a clipboard and a list of rules, or an unreasonable personal injury lawyer with ginger hair and another person's ankle sprain, or a pallid British Asian lad with a bomb in his rucksack and a selfish grudge against his fellow beings. The 'black man' has actually turned out, in many cases, to be one of the last proponents of family support, Christian charity and communal endeavour – once common standards which have crumbled like Dorset's Jurassic coast. The loss of those uniting manners is a sorry theme.

Decline is hard to deny. The funeral pyre has not just been built but is starting to smoke. Flames lick at our toes. Teenagers are killing each other with knives and guns. Illiteracy is rampant.

Loneliness is reaching epidemic proportions, not least because our churches have been so damaged by their own idiocy and by sneering atheists. Look back to that day Enoch Powell made his hated speech about 'the black man' and we can indeed say, 'Good God, whatever have we done?' – not as regards race relations, but in numerous other ways.

Some of the 'disimprovements' seem, on the surface, to be mere irritants: the reduction of informed horticultural advice in television gardening programmes which devote themselves instead to the allegedly irresistible personality of their presenters; the rise of inauthentically matey American coffee shops at the expense of older caffs; the nettle-like spread of bad language. At first we shrug off such minor blemishes but then, perhaps, we realise they represent something more menacing. If tinny little Alan Titchmarsh is the ideal of a gardener it really might tell us that, Houston, 'we have a prab-lem'.

Common sense has decayed and is starting to drop from the gum, from the ruling cadre's obsession with 'yoof' to the dismantlement of railway branch lines, or the encouragement to worship crappy modern art. There is the loss of high-mindedness in our one-time newspaper of record. It may now be more commercially aggressive but has its transformation not diminished our self-respect, our gauges of communal decency? National opinion of the police may not be altered overnight by one senior officer's crazed determination to arrest speeding motorists and to use a dead motorcyclist's image in a road safety presentation without asking his family, but once that doubt has been seeded, once this bulgy-eyed crassness has been tolerated in officialdom, how long will it be before the wider acceptance of law and order is dented? One silly hip-hop DJ on BBC Radio 1 will not, on his grotty little ownsome, bring the temple of nationhood crashing to the ground by swaggering like a Los Angeles gangsta rapper. But it nibbles at the tightrope. It scrapes the foundations. The more confused we become about our cultural identity, the weaker our national self-respect becomes, along with our very existence as a coherent society.

And weak is certainly the word for twenty-first-century Britain. National institutions cower at the mercy of an uncontrolled, publicly employed inspectorate of interfering tartars and politicised quangocrats such as snippy Suzi Leather. We subjects of the Crown have lost pride in our self-government. Propriety in public life is a dwindling resource. We have outsourced reason. We deserve it.

Who helped to build this pyre? What were they thinking? If we can identify and agree on some of the culprits maybe we can undo some of their cock-ups. Did the rot set in with the promotion of comprehensive schooling over selective education? It is too late for the generations who have passed through the 'apprehensives', but we can still make things better for their children and grandchildren. A return of academic selection to state schools is perhaps the single most practical, realisable policy to improve our country. If promotion and relegation are accepted in football leagues why should they be anathema in our schools? Anthony Crosland's ruinous work, surely, must be undone. But don't hold your breath.

Should we blame the insistence of the Thatcher Government

that personal responsibility was the be-all and end-all and that men over the age of thirty who travelled in a bus were failures? Was that the moment the idea of kindred values was ruptured? With discipline and group behaviour having been loosened in the laid-back 1960s there was nothing to restrain Thatcherism's finger-wagging expectations of personal advancement. Ephemeral enrichment, fevered by greed, was placed above long-term damage to the fabric of our nation. What did it matter if the coal miners had their noses rubbed in defeat? Forwards! Upwards! Now! Today! We are still paying for her rough-handedness.

Before we all emigrate to New Zealand, let's cheerfully admit that many things have improved. We live longer. The wrenching misery of child mortality has been sharply reduced, thank God and science (if they be different). We take more holidays and are generally less paralysed by class anxiety. Washing machines, disliked by the climate change crowd, are a wonderful invention which has reduced the domestic workload, as have throw-away plates and dogs that lick the roast beef tin.

Cities are no longer cloaked by smog and the stink of horse dung. We sleep in springier beds. Some, but not all of us, have more relaxed relationships with our children. All these are advances. So why are we not happier? What is missing?

Religious faith has declined. Secularist pulpiteer Richard Dawkins may be a fiendishly bookish fellow but he has done more to erode our substratum than anyone since Lucifer. Like many of the people who have buggered up Britain, Dawkins leads a comfortable life, cocooned in wealth and wisdom. To him it is an intriguing intellectual struggle, a paper battle played out in lecture halls and radio studios. He, like so many of his fellow false prophets, is separated from the spiritual poverty of the people whose life experiences he has diminished. Do television producers such as Peter Bazalgette pause long to consider the social consequences of their vile little programmes or are they in it simply for the money, the thrill, the creative buzz?

So much money, so many technological advances, yet such an unhappy country, so drained of community, so robotic as it staggers towards oblivion. Who landed us in this mess? Who are the halfwits, the mooncalves, the clotpolls, the pickthanks whose little touches and yanks on the national tiller steered us into such a rock-strewn channel? Read on, Macduff.

1 Jeffrey Archer

Long before Tony Blair even thought about ennobling any of the Labour Party's donors, there was talk of how John Major stamped his feet up and down on the carpets of 10 Downing Street and insisted, in the manner of Violet Elizabeth Bott until he was nearly sick, that Jeffrey Archer be made a peer. It was as bad a piece of work as Major did during his premiership and it was an early sign that places in the Upper House of Parliament were being handed out like spaces in an executive car park.

Much criticism has been fired at Blair and the Labour Party for demeaning the House of Lords. Rightly so. But this flaky combo was not the first to push dodgy friends towards the Upper House. The Archer appointment was equally troubling. That the Lords did not really take off as a political scandal until 2006 – some fourteen years after Archer first settled his bottom on the red leather benches – shows how long the British Establishment is allowed to get away with rank rum behaviour before being shamed into higher standards of conduct.

Jeffrey Archer should never have been allowed anywhere near the Lords. He was a political liability. In his earliest days as a politician he was spotted by a laconic, slightly mournful man

of the world called Humphrey Berkeley MP. I knew Humphrey a little and he had a nose for trouble. He recognised Archer as just that. His warnings to the Conservative Party went unheeded.

Archer's wild unsuitability for a Life Peerage might seem obvious now but it was also obvious to many people in 1992. There was no shortage of well-placed types who told John Major that 'Lord Archer' was a bad idea. The shadowy committee which at that time approved nominations for the Lords shed its normal discretion when the name of J. Archer came before its members. It was not uncommon, as a Fleet Street journalist during those months, to find oneself being shepherded into a corner of the Palace of Westminster's cloisters to be told off the record that 'the committee was most unhappy' and 'the committee had asked Downing Street if it was really sure about this nomination'.

And yet Archer, this scandal-flecked clown with the resilience of an India rubber ball, bounced through the trouble and straight through the stained-glass windows of the double doors which lead into the House of Lords. Maybe it was his money. Maybe it was his optimistic enthusiasm. Maybe there was another reason. But he was given that most coveted of baubles.

There he remains, despite having been convicted of perjury in 2001. The fact that he retains his seat in our legislature after serving time in prison is a smaller matter. In a way he is rather better qualified now to bring something of value to the House's discussions. Parliament needs authoritative voices and Archer certainly has some expertise now in the area of penal reform. But that is rather beside the point. He should never have been there in the first place.

It needs to be said that Archer is not an entirely bad man. He has a mercurial effervescence which can be attractive – and must especially have appealed to a Prime Minister who was surrounded by cautious nay-sayers who, he may have felt, looked down upon him. Perhaps the more the senior civil servants and the Cabinet colleagues said, 'John, you really must drop this idea of Jeffrey going to the Lords,' the more, perhaps, the idea appealed. Who can say why John Major supported Archer? But this serial fantasist, amusing company but a toxic political colleague, would have been questionable as a recruit for a gossip column, let alone for the revising chamber of our Parliament. There are times when snobbery is justified and this was one of them. Archer's crassness, his boastfulness, his social mountaineering, his pushiness, his sheer, screamingly obvious dodginess, were traffic signs to his character and should have prevented him getting as far as he did. The moment he made it in to the Lords should have been the moment our system realised that something needed doing about admission procedures to the Upper House.

Having become a producer of best-selling fiction Archer was rich. Moreover, he was generous with money. By splashing it around socially he lured journalists who should have known better. He showed how easy it is, by offering free drink and the thought of access to glamour, to subvert the British elite. At the Conservative Party conference most years, and in central London, in his south bank flat overlooking the Thames, Archer was the most flamboyant host. Invitations to his parties – champagne and shepherd's pie, a questionable combination – were greatly cherished by the impressionable and the disreputable. Lesser men and women fluttered towards Archer like moths towards an outside light in summer.

The perjury that undid him, however, showed he was not entirely a figure of fun. It related to an infamous 1987 libel case against the *Daily Star* at which Archer won £500,000. The editor of the *Star*, who consequently lost his job, later died of a heart attack. Some said that he was broken by the case – the case in which Archer lied. It was also a case in which the presiding judge, a viciously uneven beak called Mr Justice Caulfield, held up to the jury the sainted figure of Archer's wife Mary. 'Your vision of her probably will never disappear,' said Caulfield, breaking the convention that summings-up should not be biased. 'Has she elegance? Has she fragrance? Would she have, without the strain of this trial, radiance? How would she appeal? Has she had a happy married life? Has she been able to enjoy, rather than endure, her husband Jeffrey? . . . Is he in need of cold, unloving, rubber-insulated sex in a seedy hotel round about quarter to one on a Tuesday morning after an evening at the Caprice?'

It was later reported that Mary and Jeffrey Archer were hardly sleeping together. Mary Archer could have clarified matters at the time of Caulfield's summing-up. She did not.

No further questions, m'lud.

2 Kenneth Baker

Charming and mellifluous he may have been as a Cabinet minister. Some accused him of an unctuousness to rival that of nipple grease. Others forgave him his shortcomings in exchange for his delicious indiscretion. One thing Kenneth Baker could never be accused of, however, was being a mere agent of the people. There was something elevated, gamey, casually anti-democratic about him, something that made him more complicated and unpredictable than the routine-issue legislator. More destructive, too.

Baker exuded paternalistic charity yet was simultaneously hungry for headlines. This is how he came to be responsible for two ill-considered changes to our law: the Dangerous Dogs Act of 1991 and, five years earlier, the abolition of corporal punishment in England's state schools. So: unpleasant dogs could be exterminated. Whole breeds were condemned with one sweep of his ministerial nib. 'Zero tolerance', not then much used as an expression, had to be shown to canines with an imperfect grasp of discipline. But dangerous youths? Vicious children? Out-of-control schoolboys? They could under no circumstances be caned or birched or hit on the knuckles, even if they were terrorising

their classmates and persecuting their teachers (sometimes into early retirement, in one case to a violent death). And even though several members of the parliamentary Conservative Party paid good money to be treated thus in the corrective parlours of Soho!

Sophisticated Kenneth Baker, aesthete, wit and courtier, was a creature of the elite – the people who think they know better. He may have worshipped at the feet of the great Sheba, Margaret Thatcher, but he always did so with a sarcastic twinkle, sensing rightly that she was not as all-powerful or all-seeing as her sycophants and slovenly caricaturists supposed. Baker was alive to nuances of social disapproval from 'respectable' voices. He would gossip with them afterwards, behind the arras, off microphone, about the sweatier, more yeomanlike and brutish elements in the Conservative Party. He may outwardly have been loyal to Mrs T, speaking up for her until the day she was binned, but with oily Kenneth we always sensed it was a game in which he knew the party line without ever quite supporting it in his bones.

In the way that certain Wehrmacht officers in the Second World War wanted to be known as 'good Germans', Baker cherished good headlines from the upmarket newspapers which dressed to the Left: the *Guardian*, the *Independent* and parts of *The Times*. He was vulnerable to the sociologists and amateur shrinks who signed up to the anti-corporal punishment lobbies – the Clare Rayners and the Joan Bakewells and the Ruby Waxes of this godawful world. The signatories to a pressure group called Children Are Unbeatable is as good a list of *bien pensant* London as exists. They could all of them benefit from six of the best.

The caning ban came about in July 1986 when Baker was Education Secretary. It was the tightest of votes – 231 versus 230 – and would have gone the other way if several pro-whacking Tories had not been stuck in traffic and been unable to make it to the division in time. Did they chastise themselves afterwards for their failings? It is enough almost to bring tears to the eyes.

In recent times Gordon Brown has earned a reputation as 'Macavity', such is his habit of being absent at telling moments, but Mrs Thatcher was almost as bad. On the night of the caning vote she abstained owing to a dinner engagement with Nancy Reagan, wife of the US President. So much for the 'Iron' Lady. Progressive forces were delighted with Baker. Having prevented teachers from using the most effective weapon in their armoury, he then decided that they needed further training. Progressives were now in ecstasy. Ah, training! Today's all-purpose political get-out. When in doubt, when criticised, when needing to buy off a pressure group, offer more training. It creates jobs in the sector which is attacking you and it provides a line of argument to see off critics from elsewhere. 'Baker Days' were therefore introduced, shortening teachers' holidays and increasing the cost of education to the state.

Baker was also afraid of bad headlines. As a politician who fancied himself adroit in such matters, he thought he could ride the bucks and kicks of the media pony. He thought, poor fool, that he could appease the tabloid newspaper editors. The Dangerous Dogs Act followed a spate of newspaper stories about dog attacks. Freelance journalists scoured their districts for stories which could be worked up into 'another' dog-savages-child story.

Fleet Street's news editors solved the problem of what to put on the front page by deciding there was a sudden emergency of killer dogs on the rampage.

Up went the cry – invariably the wrong response – that 'something must be done'. And with Kenneth Baker in charge (now as Home Secretary, having been promoted there to get him out of the way at Education) 'something' was indeed done. Something kneejerk and pointlessly extreme. The breeding and trade of four types of dog were banned. Among them was the pit bull terrier – an animal which can be perfectly sociable, if a little exuberant, provided it has not been trained to fight. Dog experts said that Baker was mistaken. Baker was deaf to their pleas. Potentially dangerous breeds not only had to be muzzled but also had to be castrated or have their wombs scraped, and had to be fitted with microchips. Big Government demanded nothing less. Big Government should never be the Tory solution.

Inevitably it was not long before the media outcry of killer dogs had been replaced by an equally lurid media outcry about 'dogs on death row' and one particular mutt, name of Dempsey the Pit Bull, became the object of a national campaign for clemency. Cue the screech of brakes, much sudden wisdom after the event, numerous claims that 'we never intended this' and the realisation that Baker had created a publicity nightmare and a rank bad policy which did not achieve what it intended.

It is the same with his law against caning. In 1986 he assured us that caning produced more violent children. Since 1986 violence in schools has multiplied. Our streets are now roamed by feral youths who have never experienced the pain they inflict on the victims of their violence. They have never feared an adult, never been shamed into better conduct, never hesitated from a course of misconduct because they were worried about being caned. It may be only a coincidence but the demise of corporal punishment has been followed by a sharp rise in youth delinquency. Just as a majority of people, in 1986 opinion polls, said it would.

Baker, unusually for a long-serving Cabinet minister, had three constituencies in his parliamentary career. For two years at the end of the 1960s he represented Acton. Then he took over from Quintin Hogg as MP for St Marylebone in 1970. When that seat was abolished in 1983 he nested himself in the new, safe Tory seat of Mole Valley. A longer connection with just one constituency might have made him a better MP. He might have been less reliant on the patronage of the party and developed a better instinct for sensible legislation rather than the numerous grotty stews he left as his endowment to the British people.

3 Ed Balls

What makes Ed Balls's eyes bulge? This may sound like the start of a dirty joke and it is an unkind question. The poor man may have an ocular problem. He may, for all we know, have raging constipation. But bulge they most certainly do, those eyes.

Cabinet minister Balls is said to be fantastically clever, a master of strategy, a seer for the Centre Left. Despite these horizon-scanning gifts he looks permanently surprised, less the learned prophet than a man whose breakfast has just gone down the wrong way after receiving a nasty surprise from the electricity bill.

This Balls, overlord of detail, marshal of Treasury statistics, begs to be taken as a serious man of the people. Those of us who apply ourselves to that task do not have an altogether easy time of things. Apart from the over-inflated optics there is the surname – Balls! – so inviting to low comedians and political opponents. You overcome that sort of burden only by ignoring it, but Balls is good at ignoring things. He is coated in a transparent varnish which sometimes makes him impervious to other points of view and to mocking laughter. Yet we can note that his wife Yvette, who is also a Labour MP and a minister, has chosen to sail under her maiden name of Cooper. A wise call.

The Ballses are high Brahmins of the modern elite and it is their presumption, their lack of understanding for the 'lower orders' of the country they casually think they will govern, which makes them such an insufferable and dangerous menace.

Both studied at Harvard. They are economists. They used to write leader articles for newspapers with a high opinion of themselves (but rather smaller circulations) and were later crow-barred into safe Labour seats which would need little supervision. They claim vast amounts in expenses and allowances. Ed even took a chauffeur-driven government car 150 yards the other day.

Their 1998 wedding was a high-level merger, attended by the grandees of New Labour and accorded the sort of publicity which respectful chronicles of the 1920s would give the nuptials of ducal offspring. It would be easy to mistake these two for children of privilege – an impression they go to some lengths to dispel. In *Who's Who* Mr Balls lists as his recreations 'playing football, the violin and with daughter Ellie'. Mrs Balls, or Ms Cooper as we have already noted she prefers to be known, lists 'swimming, painting portraits (badly), watching soap operas'. Savour the class awareness in those two collations, the skilful elision of proletarian 'football' with intellectual, refined 'violin' and the new-mannish mention of one of his children. With Ms Cooper there is the show of modesty (the 'badly' in brackets) and then the insistence, with her soap operas, that she has a taste for populist pap on the television. Please, please, they are saying, do not think of us as aloof or spoiled. Think of us as 'ordinary people'.

With their accents, too, the Ballses seek to accentuate an unconvincing matey-ness. Ed (it is hardly ever Edward) speaks in a strangulated Mockney which manages to be both staccato and foggy. It is also peppered by delay phrases, by 'errrr' and by little stammers. So bright! Yet so ineloquent! Yvette labours for a northern twang, making her short 'a' even more aggressive when she is fighting off criticism. Few onlookers would guess that she was reared in southern England – in Hampshire, thank you – or that her husband, who loves to attack David Cameron for his public school background, himself attended a fee-paying school in Nottingham and that his father is a university professor.

This background to the Ballses sits comfortably with their political record of 'nanny knows best' interference. From the start of the Blair Government in 1997 Balls was a decision-maker at the Treasury, answerable only to his patron Gordon Brown. Many of the schemes and themes of the Brown budgets can be credited to Balls. It is not just Brown who loves complicated welfare policies which test the brainpower of the innocent citizen and clog up the machinery of government. It is also Balls. The nonsense of tax credits? Classic Balls. The anti-parliamentary shenanigans of stealth taxation, whereby clarity of tax policy becomes apparent only days after the Budget has been 'announced' to the House of Commons? Yet more Balls.

We can see his working methods apparent in the Education Department – a Whitehall fiefdom which, with classic Balls opaqueness, has been renamed 'Schools, Children and Families'. Grandeur oozing from his every pore, he announced 'the first ever Children's Plan' for British youngsters. This included the idea that all teachers in all British schools should in future be entitled to study up to Master's level at university, courtesy of the Government. Does every kindergarten teacher in the land really need to be an MA? Think of the extra costs: the money needed not only to keep teachers at university long enough for them to gain an MA, but also the higher wages they will feel they deserve once they have that title. The Ballses have a fetish for qualifications and certificates. These almost always mean higher costs to the state – and therefore higher taxes. Tsk! Fret not. The public will pay. They always do.

Cooper, who in private is said to be contemptuous of Labour backbenchers (mere elected boobies? Pah!), also has this mania for interference. She pushed through Parliament the Bill which made Home Information Packs compulsory in property sales. These 'HIPs' introduced a whole new inspectorate – an entire bureaucratic regiment which owes its existence to the Ballses and to the vast, multi-tendrilled state they feed – and have added hundreds of pounds to the cost of property transactions. Form filling, cost incurring, pointless job creating: that's the Ballses for you. This deadly duo are just getting into their stride and will no doubt be running our lives for many years to come.

After you with that cyanide, Perkins.

4 Peter Bazalgette

Television producer Peter Bazalgette is pretty upfront about it: he's in it for the money. With programmes such as *Big Brother* and *Ground Force* and *Changing Rooms* his creative imperative has not been art or journalistic exposure or some vocational belief that the electronic media might educate the population. Profits, moolah, cash, ka-ching, ka-ching. That, as one of the participants in Bazalgette's low-grade programmes might say, is what makes his todger tingle. Sod society. So long as big brother Baz gets rich.

When it comes to television Peter Bazalgette is a libertarian, opposed to regulation, impatient of convention or peer opinion. He is scornful of the idea that the viewing masses might benefit from a little light elevation and dismisses his many critics as 'snobs', 'miserable puritans', a 'cultural elite'. But as goodtime girl Mandy Rice-Davies said in the Profumo-era court case, 'He would say that, wouldn't he?' Here, after all, is a public school, Cambridge University-educated man whose income comes from trash and whose journalistic hero is . . . Kelvin McKenzie. Here is the English National Opera board director who lives in a smart house on Notting Hill and has a country

spread in the West Country, yet is happy to impose on terrestrial TV viewers the idea that a few berks crushed into a small space in the east of London somehow represent the future of modern Britain.

Screw the rest of you. So long as big brother Baz creams off his emoluments and makes his millions of quid.

Bazalgette's programmes are brain rot – highly successful brain rot, it must be said, but brain rot all the same – and they have become progressively sillier as he has become addicted to profits. In the year 2000 that process reached a socially cancerous moment when *Big Brother* was first shown on Channel 4. This is the same, publicly owned Channel 4 which was set up by the Government, and given the rare privilege of a broadcasting licence, to produce 'high-quality and diverse programming'. Bazalgette himself should know the requirements of that licence. He has been a non-executive director of Channel 4, after all, even while being one of the channel's major suppliers. Nice.

Big Brother takes a handful of odd people, mostly between the ages of twenty and thirty, and subjects them to round-the-clock filming. The age focus is one of the show's key ingredients and one of its key evils. *Big Brother* contestants limit their conversation to the narrow interests of their own age group. They seldom learn anything from their fellow inmates because there is seldom anyone noticeably older or wiser in the group.

Some of them are close to being mentally unstable. Sometimes the whole lot of them are 'celebrities', which only seems to increase the likelihood of emotional oddness. The way these locked-up creatures interact gives the programme its story. If they are polite to one another and stare out of the window, saying not very much, they are left on the cutting-room floor by the editors and do not become famous (and therefore rich). If they scream and shout and are vile to one another they receive lots of coverage and, more than likely, end up as a 'celebrity' all in their own right. Guess which option they choose.

Big Brother may claim to offer a face of 'real' Britain but in its age selections and the concentration on showy characters with an oiky attitude it is no more 'real' than stage blood. Bazalgette, with a little justification, says that the programme holds up a mirror to our country and shows us what we have become. That, however, is a disingenuous and increasingly circular argument in that it ignores the legitimising nature of TV and the fact that *Big Brother* is now helping to create this society. Once viewers have seen forms of behaviour on the telly they suppose that they must be 'OK'. When viewers listen to the gormless, profanity-laden witterings of the twenty-somethings on the TV screen they think they need not bother to mind their language or attempt to become more eloquent. *Big Brother* cements into the public imagination the idea that we really are a nation of urban, childless, sexually incontinent dullards. Bazalgette, the behind-the-scenes circusmaster, may himself be terribly civilised, with the pukka accent and flawless manners of a privileged patrician, but it is as though he is determined that no one else should be like that. It is as though he is fuelled by some destructive desire to get his own back on this ruptured society and condemn it to even greater anti-intellectualism and long-term weakness.

Bazalgette started his TV life as a researcher on *That's Life*, a show not without merit but brushed by a slightly hysterical belief in consumer rights. Was that where he plotted the downfall of these troglodytes who phoned in with their photographs of misshapen vegetables and their sorry tales of being defrauded by bad conmen? Where was Bazalgette's libertarian instinct then? Should he not have been an advocate of *caveat emptor*? That, after all, is his stance on viewers of *Big Brother*.

After *That's Life* he graduated to *Food and Drink*, the programme which among other things gave us that monster Jilly Goolden, she of the ridiculous wine descriptions as she squirted cheap vino round the back of her horsey gums. Bazalgette himself is an ostentatious gastronome yet he claimed, with *Food and Drink*, to be trying to democratise food. He is also sometimes credited with 'inventing' celebrity chefs. This is not quite true, given that Fanny Cradock was around in the 1950s, but he certainly helped to project a new breed of media-savvy cooks canny enough to ride the publicity pony.

And then came *Ground Force*, which started with a vague aim of showing viewers how to do some gardening but soon narrowed in on Charlie Dimmock's boobs and Tommy Walsh's London bluffness. *Changing Rooms* was *Ground Force*'s indoors cousin, as cheap as the modern shelving units and lurid paint colours which featured so consistently in the series. It even had a Cockney carpenter just like Tommy Walsh. Unoriginal? Yes. But as Baz likes to say, spin-offs make so much more money. Bottom line, old boy. And devil take the consequences. He may be a descendant of the man who built some of London's sewers but, as Stephen Fry has said, he is now pumping the shit back into the homes of Britain.

Both *Ground Force* and *Changing Rooms* operated on the supposition that old must be bad and new must be better. Change was a non-negotiable, and it had to be quick change. The idea that evolution might be preferable, or that craftsmanship might take more than a few hours, was absent from these frenetic, deadline-obsessed programmes. Home-owners were dictated to by experts, many of whom, incidentally, were the most appalling, modernist 'snobs' who insisted on fashion and the despotism of 'design'. Peter Bazalgette, so opposed to snobbery in TV criticism, did not mind. He was too busy counting his notes.

To call Bazalgette a parent of reality TV is not quite right because the true begetters of the trash, the sub-mental muck, the idiotic smog which passes for so much mainstream TV nowadays, are the viewers. They, or rather we, are responsible for the existence of such fare. But Bazalgette and his ilk are the midwives.

Peter Bazalgette claims that he produces 'no brow' television. Is that really a description for a show such as *Fear Factor*, in which contestants at one point had to eat horse entrails? Maybe it is. Or maybe we have become so paralysed by anti-elitism that we are foolishly reluctant to embrace the concept of snobbery. Maybe terrestrial television programmers *should* be snobs. Maybe they should try to civilise the seething, drunken, Hogarthian populace of twenty-first-century Britain. Maybe, instead of holding up a mirror to society, public TV channels should try to save, salvage, redeem and rescue their woefully under-cultured audiences. A little more judgementalism may be the only way we can repair our broken kingdom.

5 Richard Beeching

Yarde Halt, Sharpness, Wressle, Arthog; Stepney, Ainsdale, Ripon, Ince. Early in 1963 these were just some of the evocative names which appeared on a long list of railway stations to be closed. It was published by the Ministry of Transport and the headlines in the following day's newspapers read 'AXED'.

Yarde Halt, Sharpness and Co. were branch-line stations, many of them small, rural concerns which, the Ministry said, would have to be shut to make the national railway 'economical'. With one scratch of that Whitehall nib much of rural Britain lost its link with the rail network. Lines which had been built by earlier generations were ripped up and left to grass. All that toil, all those cuttings and embankments, tunnels and bridges – brushed into the bin like cold leftovers.

The list of targeted stations, in its own way as melancholy as the names on a village war memorial, was the work of an accountant known for his spacious three-piece suits, shoe-brush moustache and an unswerving belief in the bottom line. His name: Richard Beeching.

Just typing that name fills one's fingertips with rage. Dr Beeching – later, inevitably, Lord Beeching – was a short-termist dunderhead, a bean-counter to beat all bean-counters, a figures man disinclined to think beyond the end of a balance sheet. His decision to cut 100,000 jobs and to close 2,000 railway stations, along with 5,000 miles of rail track which had been built at the cost of countless navvies' lives, was one of the most anti-progressive steps of the last fifty years. To this day there are traffic jams and bottlenecks which can be traced to Beeching. Pollution is higher than it need be, thanks to Beeching. Suburban sprawl is bigger, the highlands of Wales and Scotland more deprived, and hundreds of thousands of commuters unhappier than they should be – thanks to bloody Beeching.

An early example of the time and motion man, he was a physicist (the doctorate was from the Imperial College of Science and Technology, London). After shuffling paper for the Ministry of Supply during the Second World War the always well-fed Beeching joined ICI and worked in man-made fibres. He was a member of something called the Terylene Council, whose meetings must have cooked up a right unpleasant fug in warm weather. Not that Beeching was one for sweaty man-made fibres himself. Oh no, sir! This old grammar school boy liked to cloak his chubby limbs in Savile Row's finest weeds. A proper dandy he was, in broad-gusseted trews and tailored waistcoats. A fob watch was slung from its lower quarters, the better to keep an eye on workers' punctuality. Asked once why he felt so many railway stations were dirty he replied that it was because the public were filthy.

In 1960 Ernest Marples, the Conservative Government's Transport Secretary (whose other triumphs included the introduction of yellow lines and parking meters), was talked into applying 'modern management practices' to the railways. As today, 'modern management practices' was a euphemism for 'bring in some consultants and get them to recommend widespread job losses which I, as a politician, could not myself propose'. Beeching, with his scientist's grim reductions, his abacus brain, his slavish devotion to the task, was the man for the job. He was that dread creature, a skilful committee man, a man who knew how to 'work the system' and 'get things done'. Beeching, once he had been fired from the quarterdeck, became a deadly missile. Marples had created an ogre.

Within minutes, it seemed, Beeching had been appointed chairman of the new British Railways Board. He demanded a salary to match what he said he had been paid at ICI. It was £24,000 a year, huge money for the time.

Profit, profit, profit: that was his mantra (with its offstage chorus, 'and bugger the consequences for the long-term national interest'). Never mind that no other railway in Western Europe was making money. Never mind that rail track, once ripped up, would never be relaid and that a prized inheritance from the Victorians would be lost for ever. Profit, profit, profit, barked the fat man in the waistcoat as he sat in the first-class compartment of lovely old trains up and down the land, scowling at the peasants who used them, twitching in resentment at the old-world charm of the rural stations and their communities.

Seaside resorts were grievously hit in the cuts. Rail freight was ruined for thousands of small companies. Commuters in the Midlands had their trains almost wiped out. 'Let them drive,' argued Beeching the polluter. He also invented the concept of that most depressing of lifeforms, the 'rail bus'.

This menace, this foolish, insistent slasher-and-burner seemed to revel in becoming, as he did in near record time, 'public enemy number one'. Awash in his own public-pay gravy he was determined to deny it to others. It was as though he took a perverse pleasure in his pessimistic forecasts and their ill-judged consequences.

Beeching damaged our transport network so badly that it suffers to this day from his malign meddling. He died in 1985, aged seventy-one, too early to see the late twentieth century's huge rise in numbers of rail users, too early to witness the gridlock which has come to England's roads. He never looked much of a man for saying 'sorry', but he also died too early to utter an apology for the monumental error which cost us thousands of our rustic halts and wrecked the reach of the truly national rail system, once and for ever.

6 John Birt

Two short words convey the waffling mediocrity of the British Establishment in these early years of the twenty-first century: Baron Birt.

Rubberised shoes, an Armani suit, fashionable spectacle frames, sparse hair trendily mown; between two sideburns, so silly on a man aged sixty-three, is slung a wide mouth from which stream fluent platitudes, rendered near incomprehensible by jargon. Here is John Birt, or to give him his full, corniced moniker, Baron Birt of Liverpool in the County of Merseyside.

Poor Liverpool. Think of the poets, the musicians, the brilliantly witty drinkers and amateur polemicists who have sprung from that great city's loins. Yet here is a world-class bore, raiding some of Merseyside's glory to stick in his lordly title. He should be done for trading under false pretences, if nothing else.

But there are other, more grave charges to lay at the splayed feet of this plodding windbag. He is the man who turned the BBC into a bean-counting Babel. He is the Olympian crasher, obsessed with systems and procedures and power diagrams and channels of accountability, whose idea of television journalism

is for a reporter to reach conclusions before setting out for the front line. He is also the gallumphing meddler who made it his business to inject some 'blue skies thinking' into Tony Blair's Downing Street. Ah, 'blue skies thinking' – the smart way of describing the ancient art of rotating the tip of one thumb around another, while staring out of the window, thinking of steamed marmalade pudding.

Birt the Bore spent the 1960s and early 1970s in pretty interesting company. He mixed with Mick Jagger and David Frost. This only makes his dullness all the more baffling. He has had opportunities which should make him a fountain of spontaneity. There is no excuse for Birt as he is, which is colourless, disapproving, an agent of dreariness. He is even, for God's sake, 'a friend of Cilla Black'. What on earth does chattering sparrow Cilla see in this prolix misery?

With that other world-beating buttonholer Peter Jay (who went on to become Robert Maxwell's chief flunkey), Birt wrote a series of worthy articles in *The Times* a generation and a half ago. These asserted the importance of TV journalists having a 'mission to explain'. What did that mean? Good question! But in short Birt felt that a TV reporter should, before going out with a camera, have a clear view of what he or she wanted to find. In cricket they call this sort of approach the 'pre-selected shot'. In journalism it can perhaps be called 'finding the pictures to suit your theory'.

Birt became Director-General of the BBC after managing to give enough members of the ruling Conservative Party the impression that he was a free-market man who would make life awkward for the BBC lefties. He introduced an 'internal market' which multiplied bureaucracy and forced BBC 'cost centres' to charge one another for services they had always provided without any paperwork. Result: a boom in the number of book-keepers and clerks and accountants employed by the BBC. Producers were obliged to use independent-sector facilities when they were cheaper. Result: huge numbers of BBC staff resigned, set up independent production companies, and made a mint because the corporation was no longer able to staff the facilities they used to run.

On Birt's arrival in 1992 the BBC spent £300 million on overheads. When he left a decade later the figure was £500 million. This man wasn't an agent of free-market rationalisation. He was a state megalith-maker.

Birt was also Director-General when an edict was passed round that journalists should not probe the sex lives of government ministers, even if there was a public-interest case for doing so. This was decided after Peter Mandelson was outed on screen by Matthew Parris. Birt was an old, platonic friend of Mandelson. There was no direct proof that he had been responsible for the edict – it was attributed instead to the BBC's 'chief political adviser' (now there's a Stalinist title). But if Birt had been in any way linked to this censoring edict it would have been quite wrong, especially when the Government was passing significant gay rights laws. Similarly, it would have been quite wrong if Mandelson – out of some form of gratitude – was involved in Birt being offered a position at 10 Downing Street after he left the BBC. Did Birt get his job as a personal adviser to Blair simply on merit? Of course he did! Perfidy on anyone saying otherwise. As a Downing Street policy wonk he was said to be influential, yet he was certainly shy. The idea of him appearing before MPs to account for himself at a select committee was long resisted. What happened to his own 'mission to explain'?

When Birt talks it is as though each word has been inspected for sobriety before it leaves his lips. His mouth makes a light smacking sound as he speaks, an affliction often found in those who do not drink enough (he is, needless to say, an abstemious jogger). He also wriggles his nose ever so slightly as he talks, as though his nostrils have detected some stench of inefficient management in the room. Birt affects an interest in football but it is hard to know if this is simply out of a desire to appear interesting or one of the Labour boys. He is, meanwhile, a surprisingly enthusiastic swordsman, having lost his first wife in the divorce courts after admitting to adultery. However does he manage it? Bores them into bed, maybe.

He has paid heavily to be a statist lead-weight. Soon after he became Director-General the press learned that he was in fact employed as a consultant – with all the attendant tax breaks. He was even writing the services of his wife off against tax – her services, let us hurriedly note, as a secretary. This status as a freelance was found impolitic, out of keeping with the public service standing of the D-G, and Birt reluctantly became a staff employee of the BBC. This meant he had to sell LWT shares which in turn lost him a benefit of several million pounds when LWT was sold to Granada. So: a bore *and* a loser.

But worst of all, John Birt is the prime exponent of a whole realm of management robots. *Private Eye* magazine calls it Birtspeak, the jargon of all time-wasting bureaucrats. His 1999 'Framework to the BBC Cathedral' management diagram, a classic of the genre, contained ten arrows, eight circles, five solid-lined boxes, five broken-lined boxes, and a welter of obtuse clichés. Or how about this 'BBC Broadcast Intranet Strategy Statement' from the same era? It begins:

> The Overall Broadcast Communication Strategy visions a more open and listening environment for Broadcast staff, bringing the Broadcast family closer together through the availability of timely, accurate and relevant data using a number of tools. The Communication Strategy promotes direct face to face communication as the prime manage-ment tool for delivering messages. The most significant indirect tool envisioned is the Broadcast Intranet. It is seen as a supporting mechanism to enable ongoing daily activities which will continue to be driven by the more personal delivery of strategic measures via the management structure.

Got that?

Or take this 1995 advertisement for a BBC 'Corporate Breakthrough Adviser'. The successful candidate would

> align Breakthrough more closely with business needs; support the existing network of advisers and facilitators; work with Business Unit Heads and other managers who

want to develop their use of team-based problem solving; help sponsoring managers set up teams; facilitate individual teams; deliver adviser and facilitator training; building awareness of the value and successes of Breakthrough.

Workshops, practical learning experiences, collaborative teamwork, away days, internal communications, management training co-ordinators, feedback participants, tutored skills practice – all these horrors of modern British office life mushroomed because Birt was getting away with such drivel at the BBC. When our most important national media outfit, supposed clear voice of the nation, is paralysed by such jargon, is it any surprise the rest of corporate Britain has been taken hostage by the bullshitters?

7 Frank Blackmore

Next time politicians are addressing the unlovely subject of 'Britishness' they should think 'mini roundabouts'. Is there any truer symbol of our country today?

Mini roundabouts are suburban, bossy little objects. They are imposed on us from on high, ostensibly for our own good (but just as possibly because they create work for consultants). Their introduction involves great cost and prolonged upheaval at the end of which you are left with a small lump, little bigger than an upturned saucer, on the Queen's highway.

On first consideration mini roundabouts look democratic. A passing socialist could no doubt draft a thesis claiming mini roundabouts as tools of the class war. These dented nipples in the roadway may indeed look like a device to allow 'one car, one chance'. It may seem as though they allow each vehicle to have its turn, without preferment. The phutty Ford Ka or the sagging Datsun Cherry, laden with immigrants, can have as much of a voice at the mini roundabout as the millionaire's purring Lexus. Is that not an achievement?

Be not deceived. Mini roundabouts are a menace. They are an aesthetic blot. They kill the spirit of the road. And they cause car sickness, as the pongy interior of many a family hatchback will confirm.

They were invented by a 1960s' Ministry of Transport boffin, Frank Blackmore. It may seem harsh to include Mr Blackmore in this sort of book. He was only doing his job. He was maybe even 'acting under orders', as the saying goes. But life is a merciless business. He it was who devised the equation $Q=N/t$ (in which Q is the flow, N is the average number of vehicles in the system at any moment and t is the average time taken by any vehicle to pass through the system). Do pay attention at the back of the class.

Comrade Blackmore believed that his invention would have us all zipping around town in our Hillman Imps. But did he envisage how prevalent mini roundabouts would become? Last summer my family and I spent two wet weeks in Brittany. The place has been near wrecked by mini roundabouts. Bloody things. They were everywhere. Mini roundabouts are the new 'vice Anglais'.

Blackmore created a monster, as anyone who has visited Swindon's 'Magic Roundabout' junction – a moonscape of mini roundabouts all stuck together – will agree. The mini roundabout has run amok. Mini roundabouts have replaced ancient crossroads, once site of the gibbet and the wind-gnarled oak, more recently a place of sporting judgement. At crossroads you had to time your leap, gun your engine, make tyres squeal. We could not all be Nigel Mansell but we could at least get the adrenaline pumping by darting out in front of an oncoming juggernaut. Why should only Mr Toad have some fun at the wheel?

At a crossroads, moreover, you have a sense of one road being senior to another. Should the busy A road not have priority over the piddling country lane? Not at a mini roundabout it doesn't. Heavy traffic has to screech to a halt for even just one vehicle. Mini roundabouts are the very opposite of democratic. They are the many bending to the few. We should have no truck with them.

8 Tony Blair

Thursday, 28 June 2007. It is 10.34 a.m., an hour when specks of morning dust still dance in slanting shafts of sunlight. An announcement is made to a sparsely filled House of Commons. The Rt Hon. Member for Sedgefield (Tony Blair) has 'accepted the office of Steward and Bailiff of Her Majesty's Three Chiltern Hundreds of Stoke, Desborough and Burnham in the County of Buckinghamshire'.

A wigged clerk scratches in his ledger. A couple of the Hon. Members scattered around the Chamber make lightly satirical grunts. Mister Speaker gathers the broad sleeves of his gold-hemmed gown, quietly croaks 'Order', and calls for the start of Questions to the Secretary of State for Education and Skills and his ministerial colleagues. First up is the Minister for Higher Education and Lifelong Learning, a low-wattage lightbulb burning under the name of Bill Rammell. The question, as I recall, concerns a proposed boycott of Israel by polytechnic lecturers and their ilk.

Just twenty-two hours earlier Tony Blair had been the First Lord of the Treasury. At his last Prime Minister's Questions he was given an unprecedented ovation by the entire House. Yet now, as Thursday's business proceeds, there is almost a feel of 'morning after the day before'. The news concerning Blair's instant departure certainly has a taste worthy of a hangover day. It is sour, slightly acid and leaves many people musing 'we will never, ever do that again'.

As Prime Minister, Blair was one of the few men on the planet able to order a nuclear weapons strike on a foreign nation. This Blair controlled the destiny of billions of pounds' worth of public money. He ran a vast network of patronage and official intelligence. He was a prized guest of the White House in Washington, DC. His name and image were known to perhaps three-quarters of the adult human beings on Earth.

More than any of those, Blair the International Politician was an elected Member of the British Parliament. If he had not been an MP he would not have been able to do any of his great swanking. It was from his membership of this place – this place he was now so quickly spurning – that he derived his power. Yet within hours of surrendering his seals of office he decided to quit Parliament, too. Couldn't be bothered. House of Commons? Nah.

The archaic stewardship of the Chiltern Hundreds is one of the limited number of emergency exits from the Commons. History, you see, has generally taken the view that membership of the Commons is not only a privilege but also a duty. It should not be viewed as a 'job' but as something more vocational, almost pastoral. Chiltern Hundreds' stewards, however, may not also be MPs. So at the first chance Blair had done something unmatched by his recent predecessors. He had given up on his parliamentary obligations.

John Major, Margaret Thatcher, Jim Callaghan, Ted Heath, Harold Wilson: all, after leaving 10 Downing Street, remained in the House of Commons. They felt they owed it to the place. They respected the symbolism of a premier returning to the backbenches, knowing that this emphasised the parliamentary character of our democracy and, perhaps, that it was a good reminder of the transience of power. It is from the people that politicians derive their right to make laws. To sit on the green leather benches is to represent the electors who have made their personal choice. This is why we retain a constituency system. This is why we do not have a president.

The electors of Sedgefield, naïve darlings, had voted for Blair in 2005 in the expectation that he would be their MP for a full parliament. He dumped them, just as he dumped Labour Party supporters nationally who had thought he would serve a full third term.

Had Blair remained a parliamentarian he would be obliged to disclose his outside earnings (£7 million and rising), interests and patrons. Any free holidays he received would need to be declared. Any little freebies secured by him or his wife, ditto. Then there was the tiresome business of having to attend to constituents' petitions and pleas. *Quelle* yawn. C'mon, guys. I've been Prime Minister fercrissake. Why would I want to hang around for another two to three years helping poor people with their pathetic problems and their pathetic lives? Please. I've got the chance of an international role in the Middle East thanks to my friend George Bush. Think I'm gonna turn that down, particularly given the fat expenses and a great pad in Jerusalem?

And all the money I'm gonna make?

Sir Edward Heath did not just hang around a few years in Parliament. He remained so long that he became Father of the House. Sir John Major became a forceful speaker from the backbenches. James Callaghan saw it as a matter of honour to continue serving the people who had sent him to Westminster. Later he moved to the House of Lords, where he was a regular attender, like Margaret Thatcher. Not only is Parliament strengthened by the presence of such former prime ministers. The ex-PMs show themselves to have some modesty, to be genuinely interested in the legislative process and to have the basic decency to stay with the institution which made them.

But not our Blair. Perhaps he felt it would demean him to sit on the backbenches. Perhaps he could not bear the thought of the coarse ruffians he would have to count for his neighbours. Perhaps he felt that, after the numerous measures his Government took to diminish the House of Commons, there was no point sitting in such a reduced assembly and he might as well think about running for the presidency of Europe. It was Blair, don't forget, who guillotined a record number of bills, who introduced deferred votes, who did away with bi-weekly PMQs, who got Britain to swallow the EU constitutional settlement which created the big presidential job. It was Blair who misled Parliament about going to war in Iraq, who mocked Parliament's traditions and formalities and its old-fashioned obsession with detail. Detail? Pah! That's only for weirdos.

There is a good, rough word to describe Tony Blair but we

had better not write it out here in full. Let us just say that he's a selfish w***** and that he'll be forgotten about long before Westminster vanishes from the political map.

9 David Blunkett

When obituarists sit down to assess the life's work of David Blunkett, which of his many achievements will they place in the opening paragraph? Will Blunkett be remembered primarily as the man who with two ill-considered policies helped cause the immigration explosion at the start of the twenty-first century? Was he not also the Education Secretary who overloaded schoolteachers with 'Citizenship' classes? Just as he was the Home Secretary who had the wheeze of cut-price police officers who proved to be so scared of the public that they would not even confront thirteen-year-old troublemakers. What rich pickings Blunkett has left us.

We Brits used to laugh at the police in other countries – those traffic cops chewing gum in New York City, or Spain's old Policia Nacional, lazy lumps in brown uniforms who were nicknamed *los maderos* (the logs). Italy had its dozy Polizia di Stato, caps pushed to the backs of their tousled heads as they posed beside dented blue Lancias and watched the girls go by. What clots those foreign police were. They may have worn guns in the holsters of their gold-braided outfits but they never looked as though they could stop a criminal. Only the elite

police squads had to be feared when you were abroad. The rest were a joke. Not like solid Mister Plod. Not like the dutiful British bobby.

Then Blunkett, the worst Home Secretary for many decades, had a bright idea. He was taking heat for not putting more coppers on the beat. He yearned to be able to claim that the Government had 'invested' many more millions on policing than its predecessor. And so he came up with the idea of PCSOs – Police Community Support Officers, or 'Blunkett's Bobbies'. Blunkett's boobies, more like. When these plastic Plods were born the idea of a consistently competent police force was lost.

There is a good reason police, since the days of Peel, have worn a uniform. It conveys the idea that they conform to shared standards. One for all and all for one – that sort of thing. The uniform showed that they were part of a national force with one aim. With PCSOs this idea was ruptured.

PCSOs, some of whom are as young as sixteen, receive little basic training. Unlike proper policemen and -women they are allowed to strike. They can hand out spot fines for litter, cycling on footpaths and other petty offences, but they may hold suspects only for thirty minutes. Half an hour? It's hardly long enough to get through the various holding pens of the centralised police switchboard's telephone tree. In their lookalike outfits they could so easily be mistaken from a distance for a real policeman, and yet they are nothing of the sort.

These non-rozzers are not feared by even sub-teen urchins who casually flick them V-signs or cry, 'Yeah, and wot you gonna do about it?' if a PCSO tries to tick them off for bad behaviour. There have been cases where the feebleness of the PCSOs has been more serious. In Manchester a ten-year-old, Jordan Lyon, drowned in a lake even though two PCSOs were on the scene. They were too worried about health and safety to leap in to rescue the boy. In Plymouth two PCSOs went to an educational home after a report of trouble. The officers, soon after arriving, locked themselves in a room rather than face down the miscreant, a thirteen-year-old boy. Their timidity was excused on the grounds that they were 'not trained to deal with violent confrontations'. Police Commander Chris Bourlet said that PCSOs are instructed not to 'intervene directly in violent situations'. This was after a fifty-nine-year-old woman had to come to the rescue of a middle-aged man who was being beaten up by a gang of women in London while the PCSOs stood behind a tree. One can imagine their knees knocking like Scooby Doo and Shaggy after seeing a ghost. When the woman complained about the PCSOs' inaction, Commander Bourlet said, 'It is clear . . . that the role performed by the PCSOs . . . did not meet your expectations'. It was the language of a sweet manufacturer responding to complaints about the quality of a bar of milk chocolate.

What is the point of dressing someone up to look vaguely like a police officer, and putting 'police' in their title, if they are not able to cope with a small degree of violence? Is violence not likely to be present in a large number of police situations? Given their propensity to call for urgent help at the first sign of trouble, should PCSOs not perhaps be renamed PC-SOS? That's SOS for Save Our cotton Socks.

Now to immigration. Blunkett liked to present himself as a tough-talking sort of Home Secretary, a white, working-class man who spoke the unpalatable truth and who represented rightwing Labour, shouting up for the common man. Two decisions made when he was at the Home Office were the very opposite of tough, or rightwing. In 2002 he trebled work permits for immigrants. His claim that this would reduce the number of asylum seekers proved not to be true – for a reason that should have been obvious to him. The countries producing asylum seekers were, with the exception of China, completely different from those producing applications for work permits. If there had been turnstiles at the airport arrivals of Britain they would have been rotating like the wheels of a speeding Aston Martin.

A year later, in 2003, Blunkett could have imposed a transition period for immigrants from the new EU states from Eastern Europe when they joined the following year. These are poor countries where the disparity in wages with Western Europe made it obvious (to all but Blunkett) that there would be a stampede for the low-paid jobs in Britain. Blunkett's failure to do so resulted in heavy immigration, so great that schools and hospitals in some parts of the land have been run ragged. Immigration has made the housing shortage worse. It has created racial tensions. The one thing that can be said in Blunkett's favour is that at least some of these immigrants have managed to find work as PCSOs. In more serious vein, the true beneficiaries of Blunkett's policy have been unscrupulous employers and the British National Party.

In this broken country which Blunkett's ill-guided policies have helped to create, the concept of British decency has shrivelled. Fear not. Blunkett, at the urging of his old university teacher Sir Bernard Crick, had a solution. They would be taught 'Citizenship'. These new lessons would extol the virtues of politicians and our political system (the same system which allowed Blunkett to keep a grace and favour London house long after he had left the Cabinet). These courses, for which teachers had to be taken from other subjects and trained at vast expense, would distract children from more demanding disciplines such as physics or chemistry or foreign languages, the teaching of which is at a parlous low. But since when has quality mattered in our state schools? The education system is run for the convenience of ministers. Citizenship would allow Blunkett and other Labour politicians to be able to point to an 'initiative' and thus parry criticisms. Never mind that the useful parts of 'Citizenship' were already taught in the better history lessons. It would let the political elite define desirable ideals, tell pupils they should not be racist or sexist or xenophobic. Such enlightened qualities might be spread more efficiently and interestingly by any good arts course, but that would not give the minister something to brag about.

In a rare triple whammy David Blunkett helped cock up immigration, law enforcement and education. What a guy!

10 Rhodes Boyson

Bad decisions in politics are bastards. Forgive the strong language, but when politicians realise a mistake has been made it soon becomes hard to be sure of the parentage of that decision. Which minister was responsible for such a cretinous mistake? Whose appalling idea was that? Silence all round.

One such howler was the sale of school games fields over the past quarter of a century. The National Playing Fields Association, which nowadays labours under the name of Fields In Trust (acronym, oh dear, FIT), is unable to say which particular genius in Whitehall or Westminster dreamed up selling thousands of acres of games fields. There are various candidates and various measures from both Conservative and Labour governments. But a parliamentary answer from 1981 may help us to establish at least one of the leading guilty men. His name: Dr Rhodes Boyson.

Who was this Boyson (he took a PhD from the London School of Economics and liked to use his doctorate, always a bad sign)? Well, he was Member of Parliament for Brent North, a suburban London seat. He was a former headmaster who sported a pair of ridiculous muttonchop whiskers. Boyson, who was later knighted and stuck on the Privy Council, fancied himself a blunt-talking Northerner, a rightwinger from the school of hard knocks, and something of an unlikely dandy. He tended to drop into his political arguments his experience of life from the sharp end of schoolmastering. If he addressed the electorate in the manner he must once have disciplined his pupils, that was perhaps only to be expected. Once a chalk pinger, always a chalk pinger.

This ex-pedagogue should, surely, have been alive to the benefits of school games. Surely his experience of the classroom and the school sports field had shown him that nothing calms an over-exuberant boy quite like an afternoon on the football, rugby or cricket pitch. With some shy children, some non-bookish children, games can be a lifeline. They bring out a youngster's character and can nurture a sense of purpose and general bottom. Playing fields are also the place where a teacher can connect with a child for the first time and later use that connection in lessons. Games build school spirit. Games keep children lean and alert. Games are fun and can prevent would-be truants from sloping away from school.

These things should have been obvious to any politician. Yet although the Labour Party made playing field sales a campaigning issue before the 1997 general election, sales of school land have continued, leaving increasing numbers of pupils without easy access to grass, mud and goalposts. At the same time we have seen a vast increase in teenage fatness and fecklessness. The two are related.

The legislation which made playing field sales possible was

the School Premises Regulations 1981. It set minimum requirements for playing fields in relation to the number of children on the school roll. This led, inadvertently but very predictably, to state schools and local education authorities being able to declare that land beyond the minimum was surplus to requirements. Margaret Thatcher's Conservatives were backed by the housebuilding industry. Hey presto, the Thatcher Government worked on a presumption in favour of developing such 'surplus' land.

By 2002 some responsibility for school games fields rested with a quango called Sport England but some idiot there decided that in many instances selling off playing fields was OK if new indoor sports facilities were provided. This misguided policy, until recently overseen by John Prescott in the Office of the Deputy Prime Minister, and Richard Caborn as Minister for Sport, persists today.

But the mood was set back in 1981 when Boyson was Parliamentary Under-Secretary at the Department of Education. On 16 November 1981 Labour's Denis Howell asked the Government what advice he offered to education authorities on the sale of school playing fields. The task of replying fell to our muttonchop-whiskered friend. Boyson's reply talked of the 'high cost of maintaining surplus playing fields' and enthused about how 'rationalisation of school provision in the light of falling rolls can sensibly involve the sale of surplus schools and land'. If we cut through the political verbiage this is in effect saying: 'There are not as many children at school as there were a couple of years ago. We're therefore completely unfussed about seeing games fields flogged off to developers. It should mean the Chancellor won't have to give so much to the Education budget next year. Yippee.'

Boyson was not Secretary of State. That had been the soapy Mark Carlisle, followed by the distinctly dry Keith Joseph. Margaret Thatcher, as a former Education Secretary, can also take some of the blame. But it was up to Boyson, the former headmaster, to make more of a fuss. He should have defended the playing fields of England. The fact that he did not either tells us that he was so manic a rightwinger that he thought public provision of sports fields was not important – or maybe it tells us that Boyson prized his job more highly than he did the well-being of future generations of English schoolchildren.

Take him down.

11 Gordon Brown

When did you last see the police driving around in anything but a shiny new car? When did you last see a council headquarters which was not the smartest, most overlit, swankiest building in town? When did you last hear of any public body announcing proudly that it would hope to do less in the coming year in order to save the country some money?

There is a reason Britain has such punishing rates of taxation. It is that senior politicians have decided there is no shame in extravagance. There is nothing wrong, as far as they are concerned, in spending every last penny they can – and more. It makes them popular with target groups of the electorate. It certainly creates a wider client base of dependent citizens – people who might reasonably be expected to vote for the same politicians at the next election, if only to guarantee their own subsidised jobs.

Between 1998 and 2005 the public sector swelled by 11 per cent, creating nearly 600,000 more public employees (the figures come from the Office of National Statistics, since you ask). How long can we continue to employ so many of our fellow citizens? How long should the wealth creators be expected to support these public servants, some of whom are little more than bloodsuckers?

Gordon Brown is the prime example of this sort of profligate politician who uses the state's wealth as personal vote manure. He throws all this public money out of the back of his muckspreader and hopes that it will make his share of the vote grow. Depressingly, it seems to have worked in the past. Morally and economically it is more open to question.

The man who had the cheek to invoke the name of Prudence has in fact been on an astonishing ten-year bender with our money. The only reason the British people did not notice was that Brown used such complex language and such tricksy schemes. Few of us had the time or numerical nous to understand what he was up to until it was too late – by which time John Major's warning about Labour's tax bombshell turned out to be horribly true. We cannot claim we were not warned.

Brown is well known to readers so I will not delay us with analysis of his tortured psyche, save perhaps to note that he seems to have derived remarkably little enjoyment from spending so much of our wealth. It is, however, worth drawing attention to just some examples of the waste which now runs rampant through our public sector, even while other, prized services are being cut through 'lack of funds'. Too often this 'lack of funds' is a euphemism for 'Gordon Brown doesn't approve of this sort of thing'.

The state now employs some 3,250 press officers, the cost of PR and advertising having trebled since Brown took over as

Chancellor in 1997. All this time he has claimed to be a hawk-eyed defender of the public coffers. Like hell he is.

If the Government has needed publicity officers during this period it may be because there have been such gross examples of waste in our bureaucracy. The benefits system has been a nightmare, losing £2.5 billion through various errors (and that is just the start of the cock-ups). Nine reorganisations of the Health Service have cost a further £3 billion and £2.3 billion was blown on a new HQ for the Ministry of Defence, even while the Treasury was insisting on cutting a fifth of the Royal Navy fleet, eleven air squadrons and thousands of soldiers. A few years ago Brown decided to sell much of our gold reserves. He was told at the time that he was selling cheap. Gold has since rocketed in price. Yet another rotten financial call by the supposedly austere Scot.

With his rules and systems being so complicated – almost as tortured as his own psyche – only the best brains have been able to steer the frigates of state. This has therefore meant employing fiendishly expensive consultants who in 2006 were costing £1.8 billion a year across various government departments. The good thing about employing consultants, as far as ministers are concerned, is that they are an 'off balance sheet' item politically. A consultant's cock-up cannot be ascribed to the minister. Consultants also have a very decent habit of employing ministers after they have been sacked. This is terribly handy, you will understand.

Untold billions more were blown on the tax credits fiasco, even before one counts the vast sums hosed away on the Scottish

Parliament and the Welsh and London Assemblies. Each of these examples of Great Gatsby extravagance may not, alone, seem disastrous, but added together they depict a political leadership which has lost any deep-grained concept of spending restraint it once possessed.

The Treasury's electricity bill has tripled since 2000? Its spending on stationery has risen so fast that the Tories have worked out it represents the cost of 10 million ballpoint pens? Its staff seem to think they can travel first-class when on work trips to Europe? Tush, calm down dear! These are mere coins in the big picture. But add those coins together, and consider that this petty extravagance is being displayed by the people who are meant to run our national exchequer, and it is surely not paranoid to suggest that we are in the hands of profligate, crazed wastrels – of whom Gordon Brown is the worst example. Prime Minister? Prime culprit, more like.

12 Richard Brunstrom

Police forces should be feared by criminals and supported by the respectable majority. The warped genius of the British police in recent years has been to achieve the very opposite – feared by dutiful citizens while being regarded by hoodlums and thieves as a soft touch. In this ill-guided endeavour special mention must go to Richard Brunstrom, traffic-crazed Chief Constable of North Wales Police, who has pursued motorists to the point of frenzy.

Brunstrom, a keep-fit fanatic, has said that he is 'proud' of his 'obsession' with speeding motorists. Twenty-four hours a day he will chase them, seven days a week. In his blog (why on earth should an officer of the law be paid to keep a blog?) he lovingly describes copping errant motorists on his days off – it passes the time, I guess.

Brunstrom, who wears his piety on his uniformed sleeve, argues that the high number of road deaths justifies his heavy-handed policing of the highways. Families of road accident victims no doubt support him in this view. Road deaths are a terrible waste and no one would want to belittle the shock and grief they cause. But should they become the single issue of a

top cop's career? Is the wider cause of policing well served by
manic scrutiny of every car's speed and trajectory? Is there not
a stage at which a highways patrol car can cease to be an agent
of welcome safety and start to become an instrument of resented
interference, even of underhand entrapment? A police
commander needs to have the political savvy to know when
the public's support is starting to slip.

In North Wales there are now almost as many speed cameras
as there are mountain goats. The boys in the peaked caps and
souped-up police vehicles (have you noticed that they always
have the top-of-the-range models?) certainly outnumber the
old women in national-costume stovepipe hats and cake-doilly
blouses. From Llandderfel to Tywyn on the west coast, Dinas
Mawddwy to north-flung Bowydd a Rhiw, blue lights flash
their insistent message: transgress ye not the highway codes of
the Lord (by order R. Brunstrom, honorary druid). North Wales's
Chief Constable, like some leaner version of Boss Hogg from
The Dukes of Hazzard, wants every hick auto-mo-beel jockey
in the land to know that this is Brunstsrom County, boys, so
don't you git no idee-ahs 'bout speedin'.

Were it merely young racers he was targeting there might
not be a problem. Youthful exuberance needs the occasional
check. But as so often with zero-tolerance maniacs Brunstrom's
approach also hits minor miscreants, the old, the inattentive,
among whom you will usually find the most civic-minded
subjects whom common sense would let pass with a dry cough
of caution. Common sense? That is not the Brunstrom way.
He insists on convictions. He pursues his prey with a terrier's

determination. In so doing he loosens the vital connection of trust and affection between the police and the policed, not just in North Wales but also, given his hunger for publicity, across the kingdom.

Flash! Another transgressing moped rider has bitten the dust and been copped for some petty infraction of the traffic law. Nee naw, nee naw. Commander Brunstrom's boys are in hot pursuit of another Ford Ka grannie who has committed the cardinal error of travelling a few miles per hour faster than permitted. The streets of Pyongyang know a very light regime compared to the northern reaches of the principality in the hands of Heddlu Gogledd Cymru.

Motorists who stray even a few miles per hour faster than they should can find themselves pursued like Brinks Mat robbers. One old boy, seventy-one-year-old former bank manager William Shaw, dawdled along at 39 m.p.h. in a 30 m.p.h. zone. When he was done by Brunstrom's storm troopers Mr Shaw had the temerity to criticise the Chief Constable. An infuriated police force hit back and targeted the by now baffled Mr Shaw at a special press conference (paid for by the public purse) where reporters were given detailed photographs of Mr Shaw's traffic felony. Magistrates were appalled at the police's over-reaction yet they had to proceed with a small fine and three penalty points. 'Guidelines' did not permit any other sentence.

Guidelines should sometimes be told to get stuffed. Guidelines should be rewritten, if necessary, to allow for a Chief Constable to be prosecuted for wasting his own force's time. Guidelines should be on the side of the public, not of over-mighty authoritarians who use the full powers of the state to settle piddling arguments with retired bank managers who quite properly expect their police to concentrate on burglary and violence rather than slamming down on drivers for pootling along nine miles an hour faster than is strictly permitted.

Until comparatively recently police forces were led by Chief Constables who were selected from outside the police ranks. The positions often went to retired generals or admirals, or to senior figures in the community who had a feel for public opinion. We may not restore a sense of belief in our policing until we return to that practice and keep our thumbs firmly on swivel-eyed evangelists like Richard Brunstrom.

13 Paul Burrell

To the Theatre Royal, Drury Lane, one Sunday evening four years ago for something the Victorians would have quickly recognised as a freak show. Paul Burrell, sometime footman in the Royal Household, stepped on stage with a fey smile and started to sell the last threads of a soul already heavily mortgaged to the shysters of Gutter Street.

Burrell is the soapy-mannered little podge, faintly northern camp, who has made a fortune (£25 million and counting) by capitalising on his 'life with the Royals'. He is the sometime 'rock' to ill-fated Princess Diana, the junior domestic in the Royal Household on whom the Queen bestowed an affectionate nickname, 'Little Paul'. Her Majesty's friendliness to her young servant has not been repaid. For the past ten years Burrell has traded hard on his time backstairs with the Royal Family, showing that far from being 'Little Paul' he is Big-Mouthed Paul, Big-For-His-Boots Paul, even Big Fibber Paul. The man manages the rare feat of being both disreputable and dreary. Why was he taken seriously for so long?

That night in 2004 at Drury Lane he was premiering his one-man roadshow, a book promotion project for Penguin

(which should know better). Some of the anecdotes presented as fresh disclosures were nothing better than mouldy yarns, at best apocryphal – the one, for instance, about the Queen apologising to a foreign visitor when a horse farted at Ascot. 'Oh,' says the foreigner, 'but I thought it was the horse, not you.' He actually claimed that this ancient joke was a true story. There was also one about the Queen drinking her finger bowl at a banquet to make a visiting head of state feel comfortable. Likely tale.

The audience rattled round the theatre like two dice in a saucepan. 'I'm gonna be controversial,' said Burrell coyly, before repeating well-trammelled theories about how Prince Charles will never become king because the Queen will live so long and 'it would cost them a lot of money to change the stamps' for Charles's few remaining years. Penguin was inviting us to accept the idea that just because this nasty little peacock once minced around Kensington Palace with his hands around his backside, admitting Diana's lovers to her apartment late at night, he had some purchase on high constitutional politics and foreknowledge of the longevity of fellow mortals.

We too easily forget that the Diana groupies intrude into a time of bereavement. When people are in grief they deserve more privacy than in times of happiness. A family death crystallises time, ensuring that those early days of shock remain in the memory for years. That is true of any family – even a family called Windsor or Spencer. To have that period wrenched open publicly for someone else's commercial gain, time and again, and made even more painful by the sour controversy of lies and hyperbole, must be intensely painful. Why do we permit such cruelty? Why do we reward it with fat cheques?

Burrell told his stage audience about Prince Charles's behaviour at the hospital in Paris when he arrived to inspect Diana's corpse. 'He approached me and stroked my lapel and said, "Poor old thing"', recalled Burrell. 'He went into the room where Diana's body lay. He came out visibly shaken. He hadn't expected to find what he had seen. All those years he'd neglected his wife came back to haunt him.' Burrell's sordid account was no more newsworthy than the way, after sudden deaths, first of kin are often reported to be 'devastated'. It adds nothing to our knowledge. The cliché merely reduces the dignity of the moment.

Paul Burrell is not just a symptom of this problem. He is part of it. The Diana-isation of Britain which he so lucratively encouraged has lowered our expectations of proper behaviour. Received thinking claims that the Diana story softened us as a country. The opposite may be true. It has hardened us in the sense that it has made shamefulness rarer. It has made bad behaviour more likely. After Burrell we expect less of close confidants. We are less surprised by his sort of treachery.

The man now gives credulous onlookers lessons on 'how to pour a cup of tea for a member of the Royal Family'. In the United States he flogs his own-label wine with the slogan, 'I wouldn't give my princess just anything and I won't give my American ladies just anything either.' He gives etiquette lessons. Etiquette? What is the etiquette for betrayal of principle and honour? At Drury Lane that night he criticised 'all the spiteful gossip' about Diana, apparently unable to see that this is exactly what he himself peddles.

Burrell has been driven by money. His friends claim that he was spurned by the Establishment after being prosecuted for the theft of some of Diana's possessions (a case dropped only at the eleventh hour on public-interest grounds). In his stage show he tried to play the class card, describing the alleged poverty of his childhood. 'We washed in a tin bath. I was lucky. I was the oldest so I got the fresh water. It was my fate to be a coal miner.' Instead he ended up a gold digger. The first half had ended with strains of Rachmaninov, which Burrell said Diana had often played. The saccharine poignancy of this moment was spoiled by the sound engineers playing it at the wrong moment. During the second half, which was given to questions from the audience, he became uncomfortable when asked how much money he was making out of all this. 'Are you from the press?' he asked, sharpish. 'Yes,' said the questioner. 'I'm from *Gay Times*.' This threw Burrell into confusion. He suddenly eased off, blushed, and said that lots of his friends were gay.

A strong community soon drums out its charlatans. It is confident enough of its codes and mores to say 'that's wrong'. It is a sign of how enfeebled we have become since Diana that Paul Burrell was not long ago sent packing his own valise and beauty box and placed on the first steam packet to Kingdom Come.

14 James Callaghan

On 1 March 1966, the Chancellor of the Exchequer, James Callaghan, made an announcement which changed – short-changed – the British way of life. For centuries our kingdom had maintained a quirky duo-decimal system of currency which sharpened our mental arithmetic, burnished our national identity, baffled foreigners. It had survived the Norman invasion, the Hundred Years War, plague, Oliver Cromwell, the Industrial Revolution, Napoleon, the Luftwaffe. But Callaghan, bluff old 'Sunny Jim', sly and matey, bespectacled yet glint of eye, was one atrocity too far. Heritage was trashed in the name of modernity.

Up Callaghan rose to his hind legs in the House of Commons and announced that pounds, shillings and pence had had their day. They were to be abolished in five years' time. The date 15 February 1971, when it came, was known as 'D-Day'. There had been an earlier D-Day, in 1944, but that had been about the defence of sovereignty, about fighting for our island race and its idea of how to behave. The 1971 D-Day was about caving in to outside pressure. A surrender. Feeble.

Callaghan's agreement to yield to decimalisation showed

that campaigners who bang on for long enough about their pet subject tend to get their way. The pro-decimal bores had been at it since Lord Wrottesley in 1824. He was inspired by the introduction of the decimal French franc in 1795. Perhaps he was bad at his twelve times table, too.

Because the French had gone decimal first there was always a faint hint of treachery about the decimalisation lobby. It certainly became identified closely with Europeanism, and as we know those beggars do not give up. But for Callaghan and his fellow politicians decimalisation had the greatest asset of all: it was new. It was change. And change is always an option chosen by politicians who have no other appeal to the public. It is no coincidence that there was a general election in the offing in March 1966. It was held at the end of the month and the Wilson Government was returned with an increased majority, its go-ahead credentials duly improved by the stand on decimalisation.

When South Africa went decimal in the early 1960s the insecure ruling elite of London had decided that it was time to follow suit. A pro-decimal report from businessmen and the British Association for the Advancement of Science pretty much clinched the matter. Lord Halsbury had been hired to produce a report. It, naturally, advocated the change which the political class had wanted it to recommend, that being the way government reports work.

To ease the transition to 'new pence', Callaghan set up something called the Decimalisation Board, a group of part-timers alike expert in political salesmanship and wafting public reassurance. This was chaired by Lord Fiske, a Labour Party veteran. His fellow members included Lord Halsbury who had chaired the report which recommended decimalisation to Callaghan. The board had a full-time staff of just fifty, small by today's standards.

When D-Day arrived in 1971 Callaghan was no longer Chancellor. He was not even a minister. Wilson had by then lost power (briefly) to Edward Heath. But come the dread day the country said goodbye to many cherished measures of currency. Farewell the 'bob'. Adieu, sixpence. The halfpenny was allowed to limp on for a few years more but in such a small coin that it was easily mistaken for the head of a drawing pin. It was not actually called a 'ha'penny' but a 'half New Penny'. The 'thrupenny bit' bit the dust. Florin, half crown and crown all went down the pan. D-Day brought intense sorrow to millions of Britons – I can remember my father cursing almost to the point of tears – and was, inevitably, followed by a surge of inflation as shopkeepers cashed in on the failure of customers to understand how expensive things had suddenly become. In Bristol two elderly women committed suicide, leaving a note which said: 'This decimal calculator is worrying me. I cannot understand it.' Decimalisation was a victory for the 'make it simple' brigade. Multiples of ten are easier than multiples of twelve (there were twelve pence in the old shilling, and twenty shillings in the old pound). The old penny was marked by the letter 'd', in memory of the Roman denarius, but after D-Day the penny was marked by the letter 'p'. P-Day, perhaps it should have been called. After that people talked about 'twenty pee' and so forth. It was not wildly elegant.

In pre-decimal Britain shop assistants thought nothing of doing agile arithtmetic calculations, the like of which would baffle most of us today. With our ancient coin names and our distinctive LSD we had a link back to the currency of Anglo-Saxon times. We differed from much of Europe, certainly, but we were proud to be distinct.

Jim Callaghan and the political class of 1966 thought otherwise, alas. Damn them.

15 Alastair Campbell

Edvard Munch captured for many the idea of a scream. Leonardo da Vinci's Mona Lisa, similarly, catches everything in a certain type of smug poise. So how would an artist catch, on canvas, the human scowl? Well, he or she could simply paint the face of Alastair Campbell.

Dear old Alastair. In his journalist days he was a convivial rogue, a tilter against corrupt authority and an enthusiastic pricker of Establishment egos. No doubt he thinks that since he crossed over to the other side he has done a Prince Hal and has left behind his disreputable former muckers. In fact he has simply joined the complacent, bloated apparat of the political elite. He has become 'one of them' – and the tragedy is that he cannot see it.

This new Campbell is a bad hat on many counts. He is not as important as he thinks, nor as clever. His behaviour has been so blatant that he has damaged those he has tried to serve and has ended up doing far more damage to the Establishment by joining it than he ever did when he was one of its lustiest critics.

This Campbell helped drive Tony Blair hard towards the Iraq War, collaborating with intelligence collator John Scarlett to

present a hawkish view of the evidence and create a media climate in which war would be acceptable to the electorate. The truth was smudged, shorn of conditionals, baked like a conker.

As press chief at Downing Street during the first part of Blair's premiership he bred red herrings at such a rate they could have colonised the North Sea. Although he now has the laughable cheek to accuse the press of distorting facts, his media operation at Downing Street was notorious for shading stories, for twisting reporters' writing arms and for using every howitzer at his command to blow critics to smithereens.

As a cog at Downing Street Campbell was not as vital as he might have thought. He was not elected. He had less idea of the concerns of the 'ordinary man' (as he liked to say) than the average backbench MP. He was rich, privileged, metropolitan – all things he professed to regard with suspicion. He was a creature of the media, which again he loved to attack.

The reason he demands inclusion in this book, however, is something in his nature rather than in his political actions. It is his fanaticism. Campbell was – is – a deeply unBritish character. The level of his devotion to numerous causes marks him down as doctrinaire, a zealot, a bigot, a Pharisee; and all this in a man who liked to say 'we don't do religion'.

Campbell, who claims to be that odd thing, a devoted atheist, should have been born Chinese. He would have enjoyed the stricter behavioural code found in Peking and its political elite. It is not hard to imagine him at a gathering of the people's congress, clapping robotically after Comrade Someone's speech. All right, a few cosmetic changes would need to be made. We would have to chop off his legs by a good foot or so, remove his Roman nose, exchange his semi-Yorkshire vowels for something more mandarin, and kit him out with a more sanguine consort than his intemperate popsy Fiona (default setting: hopping mad). But that sort of one-party state would suit Campbell. If ever Mr Hu is seeking a spin doctor, Campbell would be worth a call.

Such vehemence of belief you find in this man. Such fervour of support. Such absence of doubt. It is unnerving, unnatural, the product, I'd say, of deep unhappiness. The reason it matters, and the reason he comes into our rifle sights, is that he infected our public life with this fanaticism. As Downing Street's second most feared civil servant (second after Tony Blair's chief of staff Jonathan Powell) he set precedents which were noted by other Whitehall employees and were taken as the new way to behave. Other ministerial special advisers started to style themselves as 'mini Alastairs'. Other information officers attempted to duplicate his system of all too transparent favouritism and retaliation. Campbellisation started to corrode the British government machine, to the sorry point we reached when Jo Moore, special adviser to Stephen Byers, tried to capitalise on the 11 September terrorist attacks in New York City to 'bury bad news'.

Campbell was total in his hatred of Tories (even though his master, Blair, was arguably more Tory than many Conservatives). He was unyielding in his devotion to Labour. He was unswerving in his work. He jogged, maniacally. He was never slightly put out, or mildly interested, or so-soish. Campbell was a man to be 'totally gutted' or 'absolutely gobsmacked' or 'utterly furious'. He supported Burnley Football Club to all ends of the Earth. He first drank like a madman, then drank nothing at all. He picked fights, screamed, swaggered, strutted, punched, clenched his cheeks and fists, hurled abuse, tore into opposing points of view. There was little about him that was moderate or restrained.

Fanaticism is seldom worth the effort. The sheer effort involved in being a fanatic makes it the most frightful fag. Many of us, sure, support a football or rugby or cricket team, but we do not mind altogether if it loses from time to time. We do not beat our breasts and howl at the new moon. Most of us can generally see the other point of view. Many of us can even bring ourselves sometimes to laugh at Alastair Campbell, which is not something he has often done. But while he was in Downing Street, and while he was pushing his views down the public throat in TV studios, and touring the country with his stage show, and promoting his grievances in book form, he spread through our land the germ of totalitarianist vehemence. It is something we could – generally speaking – do without.

What a very considerable relief, as his old enemy John Major might say, that he is no longer troubling the scorer.

16 Anthony Crosland

Galloping egalitarianism has made few mistakes more destructive, more thumpingly counter-productive, than the introduction of comprehensive schools. Comprehensives first appeared in the 1950s but their greatest champion – the man who well and truly buggered up the lives of millions of British children, their parents and teachers – was suave, intellectual, libidinous Anthony Crosland, raffish darling of fashionable London and its progressive salons.

What a piece of work Crosland thought he was. But what a prize prune he proved. It was during Crosland's time as Education Secretary from 1965–67 that comprehensives received their biggest push. Administrative time lags being what they are, this meant that the Education Secretary who presided over the most openings of comprehensives was a certain Margaret Hilda Thatcher (a fact her fanatics seldom choose to publicise).

If only Crosland hadn't been so bookish he might have understood the magnitude of his mistake. As it is, he went to his grave sourly convinced that his policies were right. Sewn as tight into his certitude as a tobogganist into his thermal skimpies, he reportedly swore that, 'If it's the last thing I do

I'm going to destroy every f***ing grammar school in England and Wales and Northern Ireland.' He didn't quite manage that but he did manage to destroy a fair few of them, not to mention the secondary moderns which were reconstituted in the new comprehensive mode. Crosland was not quite the nuclear bomb on grammars that he liked to think but he still didn't leave that many standing.

Crosland was an Oxford don. Oxford dons are seldom terribly worldly and even less commonly will they admit that they are wrong. Oxford dons rarely have much idea of how to educate dimmer brains. They tend to view the world though the blinkers of principle and theory. The theory of the comprehensive school was that every child would have an equal start in life and that every school would offer the same opportunities from start to finish, irrespective of the youngster's background. This was plainly dotty, if only because the classroom is only a small fraction of education. Education happens at home, on the way to school, on the games field, in the corridors of the school and most of all in the family. If Crosland had been true in his politically driven zeal for equality he might as well have said that he intended to 'destroy every f***ing family in England and Wales and Northern Ireland'. That is the only way he would have completely flattened the field. Instead we had to leave that challenge to Roy Jenkins, whose divorce legislation helped wreck hundreds of thousands of homes. And still Jenkins was acclaimed as a social do-gooder and as a civilised man!

'Tony' Crosland, similarly, remains one of those revered figures, his name invoked with false familiarity rather in the way that so many people, long after Churchill's death, spoke with unconvincing chumminess about 'Winston'. One of the chief reasons Crosland's reputation has endured is that his widow Susan, a glamorous American, has remained in London to strike elegant poses and raise an imperious eyebrow at anyone stepping out of line. Mrs Crosland is an old-fashioned Baltimore broad with an accent posher than found on most modern English aristocrats. She has championed her husband's memory and few people like to upset a widow, particularly one with great cheekbones, a clever tongue and access to the lunch tables of certain editors on Fleet and Grub Street.

So 'Tony' is still held to have been a visionary, a leveller of opportunity, a noble man who was taken from us too early. Selective schools, few of which remain, are spoken of pejoratively. The received attitude, certainly for the past eleven years since Labour has been in office, has been that selection is immoral.

Quite the reverse is true. Quite the reverse, in fact, is essential if we are ever to produce world-beating children in sufficient numbers to protect our national interest. Politicians lie about school exam results and claim that we have never produced cleverer, better-educated youngsters. Do you know anybody who seriously believes this? The only person I can think of in my very vague acquaintance who does swallow this laughable claim is Polly Toynbee. Other leftwingers in my circle say that they know today's schoolchildren are disastrously ill-served by Crosland's comps, 'but it is politically impossible to say anything'.

Selection is normally discussed only as something that makes life better for the few. This is wrong. Nearly everyone can benefit from selection if it is done well because it places children in their ability group, giving them a better chance of coming top in that group and feeling that they have achieved something. As the father of children who do not seem to be particularly academic, I am much happier when they are competing against a class of their intellectual equals rather than against a form full of young masterminds. How, in a class of forty, is a teacher expected to engage the brightest while at the same time explaining difficult ideas to cheerful thickos? It's astonishing that Crosland could not – or, more likely, would not – see this problem.

Our state schools have been a stagnant pond for too long. Private schools, which were fading fast during the high years of the grammars and when Crosland was Education Secretary, have never been busier. Crosland's stupid system, driven by a vindictive hatred of elitism, has only increased the gap between rich and not so rich. State schools are not getting the sparkier minds which used to buoy them. Crosland's social engineering has done the very opposite of what he intended. If he wasn't already dead it would be tempting to strangle the idiot.

17 Richard Dawkins and Charles Simonyi

Today in Britain, as on every other day of the week, many hundred homes will be visited by that dank-fingered creditor Death. This very hour, somewhere on our shared island, women stand stunned by sudden loss. Men wring their wits at what has come to pass. Youngsters hover nearby, puzzled, frightened by the clamour of grief.

In sorry scenes across the kingdom weeping adults will lift their breasts to a sensed but unknown God. They will apply their hopes to an imagined Heaven. In more cases than not they will pray. The machinery of supplication may not have been used for a while. It has often become dusty, rusted, like the workings of a forgotten bicycle bell. But pray they will and after a few minutes a note or two will usually sound from that long-neglected bell. It will comfort them. In the most miserable bleakness prayer can offer the sliver of light which, from the landing, a five-year-old frightened of the dark detects through the crack of its bedroom door.

Richard Dawkins would have none of this. Anti-religionist Dawkins, the best-known English dissenter since Darwin, is the merciless demander of provable fact. He tours the world –

generally in considerable comfort – lecturing the elites of the West that they are stupid to believe in any god. He proselytises against the proselytisers, most of his targets wishing they had a fraction of his apparent certainty. In his insistence that he is right Dawkins pushes his fingers and fulminates, outwardly still the civilised Englishman but dialectically as steadfast and immovable as any mullah. Beaky, hawk-eyed Dawkins is the suave ayatollah of atheism, accusing 'dyed-in-the-wool faith heads' that they are 'immune to argument'. As though argument was all.

But would you expect anything else from a man who owes his privileged position to a landless computer technician whose idea of fun is to ride the oceans in a *faux* gunboat and blow millions of pounds getting himself propelled beyond the atmosphere as one of the first space tourists? Dawkins holds Oxford's Charles Simonyi Chair for the Public Understanding of Science. The professor is always challenging us to ask questions, to probe, to strike a sceptical air. All right, then, matey. Who the hell is Charles Simonyi? What business has he to encourage this anti-preacher whose sermons are designed to erode churchgoing and, with that, weaken our happiness?

Simonyi, it turns out to little surprise, is an extremely rich man. Rich people generally have less use for God than their poorer fellow creatures. When your life has been a material success and you can buy the best medical care, the best food, the most temperate houses and the freedom to work the hours you choose, petition and entreaty and ragged beseechings are hardly necessary. You generally just buy what you want.

Like many rich men this Simonyi (a Hungarian émigré, he lives in North America) likes to name things after himself. In addition to the Charles Simonyi Chair for the Public Understanding of Science at Oxford University there is a Charles Simonyi Professor for Innovation in Teaching at Stanford University in California. There is a Charles Simonyi Fund for Arts and Sciences which supports certain ventures in the northwest of the US. His lordship's house in Washington State is called 'Villa Simonyi'. He has reportedly been stepping out recently with Martha Stewart, but at the time of writing he has yet to persuade her to take his name. It can only be a matter of time.

Simonyi used to work for Microsoft and Bill Gates, whom many computer geeks regard as a near deity, if Comrade Dawkins will permit that word. He was largely responsible for the creation (dread word) of Microsoft's 'Windows'. It must have given him a great sense of control over the destinies of his fellow men. No doubt he was the recipient of regular hosannas and adulation from his fellow executives and from an admiring business community. These days he runs his own company, rich enough to qualify for the Forbes list of (dollar) billionaires and to commission a yacht called *Skat*. It is decked out in the colours of a military vessel and, from a distance, could easily be mistaken for the oceangoing headquarters of a James Bond villain.

This, anyway, is the patron of Richard Dawkins. This is the man whose generosity we can thank for Dawkins's Oxford title, a handle which brings him international esteem and lends his denunciations that extra oompf, that little *je ne sais quoi*. The

'Charles Simonyi Professor'! Is there not a hint of the Old Testament or the Huguenot sage about that name? Is it not a handsome bauble to have? Gosh, we must take this Dawkins even more seriously. We must give him the gold rope and red carpet treatment. We must invite him to deliver an important lecture rather than offering him the book-signing session with peanuts and warm white wine with which other non-fiction authors must be content.

If Simonyi is, like Dawkins, unimpressed by the claims of anything but science, why does he like to publicise his name so much? Is the gratification of vanity a proper scientific activity? Surely it has more to do with the hope of cementing your name in history, of being remembered to the glory of your heavenly soul. The truly clinical, empirical scientist would not trouble himself with such baubles. He would merely give his money to the cause and wave aside the acclaim of his fellow mammals, knowing that our presence on this revolving globe is but a blink in the vast, pointless universe. As it is, his agent Dawkins dispenses despair and mockery in equal measure, promulgating doubt, complicating life for the thousands of good clergy who attempt to minister to the nation's woes. Secularism, the creed of the selfish and the short-termist, infects our body politic. The great cathedrals of England are left to rot, under-supported by a sceptical state. The social network of rural parishes withers, undermined by Dawkins and his collects of negativity. The shires' belfries fall silent.

As for the self-worshipping Simonyi, was that little jaunt into space on a Russian rocket called Soyuz TMA-10 simply an exercise in scientific curiosity? Or was our billionaire engaged on what we might call a checking voyage? Was he making sure there was no sign of St Peter jangling his keys to the pearly gates up there in the black-treacle yonder?

There is, in the heavy championing of science seen from Dawkins and Simonyi, a strange lack of humanity. It supposes that we will all want to share the belief in hard, factual science, let alone that this might help the development of a happy and calm society. It ignores the emotional needs of the poor and distressed, man's centuries-old spiritual hunger, the quest for comfort beyond material concerns. A billionaire who was less obsessed with himself and with the narrow calculations of men in white coats might think of the scenes up and down our land today. He might realise that religion, although never offering proof of God's existence, can sugar catastrophe and brighten chasms.

In times of turbulence the human being is little different from the vole or the dormouse. It will take shelter where it can. No amount of superior lecturing from an anti-Christ, not even one with so important a title as Charles Simonyi Professor for the Public Understanding of Science, will alter that.

18 Diana

Some faint hearts clutch their necks at the idea MI5 bugged Princess Diana but our Government would surely have failed in its duties if it had not followed the 'People's Princess' and listened to her conversations very closely indeed. The woman was a liability, a soufflé of false ideas, a super-model with all that that entails. She was the glamorous tool of cleverer men, a plaything for the powerful, a delusion worshipped only by the impressionable.

The Princess may have been a loving mother. That should have been enough of an achievement, surely. She may also have been photogenic and been able to convey an easy charm, providing hope for the plumper specimens of the office typing pool as they wrestled with their low-cal diets and desultory routines. But the sorry truth is that this adored concept, this packaged, airbrushed Diana, weakened our society. She made us more neurotic. As a fox will spread mange so did Diana propagate insincerity. After Diana it became so easy to emote that it was hard to tell if people meant their tears or if they were simply trying them on. Diana robbed us of the stoicism and understatement which had served Britain well. Had she not been the daughter of an earl we could say that she was an

alien doing hostile work behind enemy lines, but given that her birth and breeding were English – very English – we have to deduce that she was an unwitting virus, coring outwards to the detriment of her country and culture.

Shakespeare's *Hamlet* ends with Fortinbras saying that the fallen prince, had he lived longer, would have proved most royal. Had Diana lived longer she would likely have gone the other way. She would have exploded, or imploded, or done whatever it is that celebrities do when they run out of media sympathy. At some point she would have made a mistake – maybe a lover so vulgar that not even her groupies could have stomached the spectacle, or maybe some financial association which soured and dragged her brand into disrepute. That may even have been happening during those last days with her affair with medallioned Dodi Fayed. Shortly before her death there was a slight hint that the media cycle was about to move to its next phase – when it becomes more aggressive and starts testing its subject for flaws. Many of the photographers following her had lost respect for their quarry. The aura of the 'special' Diana, of Diana the superstar, of Diana the wronged goddess, was fading. Had she lived to see the January of 1998 it is unlikely she would have enjoyed quite such a good press.

Diana was dim. A long line of herbal-cure fraudsters, psychobabbling self-esteem preachers and emotional intelligence shysters beat a path to her palace door. She fell for them as readily as did the Prime Minister's wife, Cherie Blair. Whereas Cherie was laughed at, and rightly so, for being a nincompoop and a dingbat, Diana was feathered by sighs of sympathy, indulged simply because she looked pretty and helped to sell newspapers and magazines. If Cherie Blair had not had such fat ankles perhaps she, too, would have been indulged by the public and its press. Perhaps.

Diana weakened our monarchy almost to the point of rupture, as was clear in the week after her death when public hysteria generated an ugly mood against the Queen and Crown. That hysteria would have been impossible had our society not been sapped by vapid Diana worship. Supporters of the dead Princess spouted – and some of the unhappy creatures continue to spout – the most venomous theories about her enemies in the Royal Family. They are as hooked on tall tales as the lunatics who suggest that Nasa never landed a spacecraft on the Moon. Their anger and bitterness are astonishing, not least given that their fallen heroine built herself up as such a walking beatitude, such an adherent of positive thinking good-energy vibes. Where are the good vibes in accusing the Duke of Edinburgh of wanting to murder his former daughter-in-law? Or in libelling little Tiggy van Winkle, the Princes' nanny, by suggesting that she was plotting to marry Charles? About as absent as any evidence, I would suggest.

Had it just been a question of selling newspapers and magazines it might not have mattered. Who am I, a newspaper journalist, to deplore snappy front pages and shrewd editorial judgements? But Fleet Street went several multiples too far. It lost a grip on morality and truth and failed to hold the increasingly flimsy Diana to account. A little more journalistic rigour might have saved her from taking up with the dismal

Dodi. We heard her criticise land mines but did we hear her, when she had the attention of the American media, criticise the Irish Republican terrorism funded by the US? We heard her depict herself as put-upon, as one of the little people, but was she herself not a child of extraordinary privilege? And why did she have to lead such a splashy, extravagant life? Fleet Street colluded to make Diana think better of herself than she should have done.

Princess Diana robbed our country of its restraint, of its phlegmatic common sense and dependability. Thanks largely to her we have become a country in which the words 'crisis' and 'disaster' are devalued from overuse, a country of emotional incontinence where adults will weep if they fail to win a talent competition, or fan their mouths and shriek if they win, yet where no one bothers to welcome home soldiers from a war zone. Diana displayed welcome mercy to Aids sufferers and to little girls orphaned and disfigured by land mines, but she nearly always knew where the cameras were and she played up to their lenses like the fattest ham in the butcher's deep freeze. She escaped mockery only because she was a female 'victim' and because she was a member of the Royal Family – the very family she decided she could tolerate no longer.

We can blame Prince Charles for marrying her. We can blame the Queen for not being more canny and for not realising how the politics had changed. But Diana was a danger to the stability of our kingdom. She mixed in circles that were disreputable and, in some cases, neurotically anti-British. Any woman of discretion would have avoided these social vultures, these over-cologned new best friends with their absurd Mercedes limousines and their filthy sense of show.

Her death was shocking, horrible and a waste of beauty. But poor, unhappy, ill-guided Diana was a naïve menace, an odd mixture of simpering shyness and galloping egomania. God rest her soul, she was a mirage, a false harbinger of egalitarianism, and we were foolish ever to think otherwise.

19 Greg Dyke

The overriding condition of the British people is not wickedness or gluttony or envy, nor even, despite strong evidence to the contrary, of roaring, beery, shouty, vomit-flecked intemperance. It is tiredness. We do not sleep enough. The sleep we do take is seldom as deep for as long or continuous as it should be. We are just plain knackered much of the time.

Board a commuter train any morning of the working week and count how many heads are pushed back, mouths open, eyes shut. Ride the same train in the other direction at the end of the working day and faces will be wan, cheeks drawn, stares hollow. Tiredness afflicts us as never before in peacetime, causing irritation, accidents, illness. When weary we tend to eat more junk food rather than taking the trouble to cook with fresh ingredients. When 'done in' we not only snap at our children but also take the easy option of placing them in front of the computer screen rather than reading to them or accompanying them on a walk. The next generation suffers for our tiredness.

It shouldn't be like this. As a society we are rich and healthy. We have gadgets to do many of the household chores which sapped the stamina of our ancestors, from washing clothes to

drawing water. Motor cars save us the trouble of walking to school or work. There are supermarkets to reduce the labour of shopping. There are 'coal flow style' gas fires which do not need to be brushed clear of ash every morning amid much clanging of metal pails. Some of us even employ cleaners. Meanwhile, mattresses and pillows have never been more comfortable, or so the advertisements tell us, and draughts have become a rarity in all but the most poor – and, as it happens, the most aristocratic – bedrooms. So why are we tired? Why do we not use our common sense and indulge ourselves by sleeping for longer?

Greg Dyke. That's why. Or rather, that's who. Dyke is the man who stole our sleep.

Pint-sized Greg is himself so packed with energy that he could be one of those overpriced oat and raisin bars sold by the more go-ahead types of newsagent. He is a lively Londoner, cocksure, not much inclined to realise that there are large parts of the country which not only do not resemble Greg's beloved Brentford but also live to a different schedule. It was this lack of understanding for the 'other' Britain, the Britain of the regions, the Britain of quiet, Murray Mint-sucking introspection, which allowed Dyke to make his biggest mistake while he was Director-General of the BBC. I do not mean his admirable defence of Andrew Gilligan in the David Kelly affair – a matter which led to the Hutton Inquiry and to Dyke honourably losing his job. The decision I'm referring to was of far greater consequence. It was his insistence on moving BBC1's main news bulletin of the day back an hour, from 9 p.m. to 10 p.m.

The Nine o'Clock News used to allow you to take the dog downstairs, switch off the lights, clean your teeth and be in bed by 9.45 p.m. Prayers. A quick chapter of P.G. Wodehouse, perhaps. A dutiful good-night to the wife, if relations were sufficiently cordial. Then lights out and away with the fairies before Radio 4 had a chance to issue its pips and Robin Lustig came on with *The World Tonight*. Give or take a little, that was the routine millions of us followed for years – a routine which allowed us nine hours of sleep before reveille at 7 a.m. And for years Britain cantered along perfectly cheerful, often overworked but normally sufficiently rested.

Director-General Dyke had to go and fiddle. He pounced in August 2000, shortly after taking over the BBC. His rival on terrestrial television, ITV, had just, very stupidly, killed off *News at Ten* with its bongs and middle-market melodrama. ITV's news was now being shown some nights at 11 p.m. Not all nights, though. The lack of certainty about its place in the TV schedules earned it the nickname 'News at When'.

Dyke, himself a graduate of commercial television, felt that he had to compete for ratings. He knew that if he pushed to bring old news back an hour he could use feature films in BBC1's main evening slot. He could reduce ITV's profits. He could win! The ideas of public service, of the BBC's charter commitments to Reithian ideals of education and information and most of all to letting the poor, knackered folk of Middle England get sufficient zeds, were overlooked in the name of ratings. The news was parked an hour later, at 10 p.m.

As a result of Dyke's tinkering millions of us now go to bed an hour later. When the change was introduced there were predictions that viewing figures would drop. That has happened to some extent but the rest of us have simply soldiered on for another hour every night, waiting for the routine of simpery Fiona Bruce reading the news before bed.

ITV recently scrapped its 10.30 p.m. bulletin and restored *News at Ten*. What a pity they didn't plump for an hour earlier. Imagine another 300 or so hours of sleep a year. That is what Dyke has taken from you. Some of our children used to watch the 9 p.m. headlines, but they are now in bed by the time of the main evening bulletin. The old habit of watching the television news as a family has been eroded. Yes, children can see the news on the Internet or on BBC News24 if they are that interested, but another little bit of social glue has gone. And all because the man who invented Roland Rat wanted to muck up ITV's ratings.

20 Sir Alex Ferguson

One of the many clichés of sports journalism is to call matches 'crucial'. It is usually soccer matches that are described thus, as in 'England's crucial World Cup qualifier' or 'Wanderers' crucial relegation battle against Athletic'. Cricket and rugby players may face just as many fixtures that can decide the success of a season. The same probably can be said of field hockey or Eton fives or competitive tiddlywinks. But their games do not seem to be quite so frequently described as 'crucial'. Why is this?

This sloppy new meaning of 'crucial' sits well with the multi-billion-pound business of English soccer, a rapacious, hysterical, over-indulged world in which the most bug-eyed and discordant figure is the manager of Manchester United, Sir Alex Ferguson. What a horrible man he is.

There is little that is pretty about 'Sir Alex', as the respectful dweebs of BBC Radio 5 Live call him. Labour Party goons who normally resent giving knights or peers their 'handle' somehow always remember to speak of 'Sir Alex'. How easily we have been persuaded to accept the idea of a mere club soccer manager being knighted. 'Sir Alex' might once have meant Sir Alexander Fleming, who discovered penicillin, or Sir Alexander Mackenzie, a great

explorer of the North West Passage, or, in West Indian homes, the Right Excellent Sir Alexander Bustamente, first Premier of Jamaica. But now 'Sir Alex' refers to a cross-tempered former footballer (not a terribly good one at that) with a violent tongue and an autocratic manner, a man who has helped to drive the fun out of football and who often seems to forget that the contest on a playing field between two teams of eleven lads is merely a game, not a struggle between right and wrong.

Ferguson, who can even make the habit of chewing gum look aggressive, is so imbued with fury that sometimes the skin of his face seems to boil. He has an oddly spotty complexion for an adult. It is as though the crossness is bubbling up within him, forming little pinpricks of pus-filled soreness on his nose and chin.

He is feared by his players, feared by the press. When he is interviewed after a match he is seldom tackled low by the journalist asking the questions. How often is he quizzed about his bad behaviour on the touchline, about his intemperance to referees and linesmen, about the antics which have repeatedly seen him despatched to the stands and forbidden from standing on the touchline? The commentators have learned that anyone who dares to cross 'Sir Alex' may be banished. Feebly, they cave in to his bullying. As for the players, they know that their 'guvnor' has in the past reacted violently. He is said to have kicked a football boot at David Beckham in the changing room. Teacups have allegedly been thrown during half-time 'chats'. Ferguson is prone to baleful, close-up bawlings-out, so hot that they are known as his 'hairdryer' treatment. Ugh. The thought of all that halitosis.

This is the calibre of the man who was deemed worthy of a knighthood by Tony Blair's Mephistopheles, Alastair Campbell. It helped that Ferguson was prepared to speak publicly about his support for Blair's Labour Party. Campbell and Blair valued greatly that endorsement. They sensed, probably correctly, that soccer was the spirit of our dim-brained, sloganeering times. If they could get the pre-eminent soccer manager to support them they could reasonably hope that many of his team's hundreds of thousands of fans would follow him, or at least feel better about the Prime Minister and his entourage. Soccer, a simple and enjoyable game, was turned into a political instrument. Few seemed to mind that modern football, with its decadent pay deals, was far from any notion of socialism. We will not comment on the underhand character of many transfer arrangements – and there is no evidence to link them to Ferguson – but it was certainly rum to see a man who was prepared to pay such vast wages to a handful of star players offer his support to a political party which swept to power by attacking the 'fat cats' of the business world.

When Manchester United declined to enter the FA Cup one year it was Ferguson who was said to have formed the view that the game's oldest, best-loved cup competition was expendable. Money-making was more important to United. Should the FA Cup – offering the small club a chance of glory, as it does – not have appealed to his alleged socialist instincts? Or was it simply that this bloated egotist could not give a stuff about the lower reaches of the game and that he considered himself and his club to be far bigger than anything so meagre as 'the spirit of the game'?

Alex Ferguson. Not as nice as he looks.

21 Maurice 'Maus' Gatsonides

British officialdom is seldom happier than when issued with a new gadget with which to make the citizenry's lives more miserable. The daddy of them all, in the 'gotcha' gadget world, is surely the roadside speed camera. And the daddy of the speed camera? A Dutch rally driver, of all things, name of Maurice Gatsonides.

'Maus' Gatsonides in fact invented the thing to help him go faster. He wanted to improve his technique around corners and came up with the idea of a camera which would tell him how fast he was entering a turn, and how fast he left it. Almost ever since then speed cameras have been driving the rest of us round the bend.

It seems to have been at least partly successful in making Gatsonides a fast driver because he won the Monte Carlo Rally in 1953 (by three seconds) in a Ford Zephyr. Bill Mackenzie, a *Daily Telegraph* motoring writer, acted once as Gatsonides's navigator for the Alpine Cup in 1951, in a Jaguar XK120, but swore afterwards that he would never repeat the exercise – it was simply too frightening to be driven by such a speed maniac. Gatsonides excelled behind the wheel of snorting roadsters such as a Frazer Nash or an Aston Martin, an Austin Healey, Maserati or Porsche. It seems some sick joke, a propagandist triumph (as far from one of his beloved Triumphs as you can get) that his name should now be associated with those flashing traitors of the highway, those monocular sneaks which pop and snap at the rear number plates of zipping vehicles.

When not hurtling down the track in Le Mans or attempting the Mille Miglia, Gatsonides invented a handful of cars, chubby-faced, sleek-tailed things named Gatsos. Unlike their inventor round a hairpin bend, they never took off. Gatsonides lacked the financial backing to keep his ideas in production and the car-making concern went out of business in 1950. The old boy died in 1998 but his memory lives on, not least in the minds of Britain's persecuted motorists.

As with all mechanical threats to civilisation, happily, human inventiveness has fought back. The Internet now offers sites which betray the location of speed cameras on nearly all the roads of Britain. Dashboard fuzz-busters can be bought which groan or squeak or vreeeep when your car is approaching one of Gatso's tin sentinels. This Dutch-invented Big Brother may be watching us but we are increasingly wise to the event, ha ha! Speed cameras have given birth to a whole new seam of expertise for pub bores, men who can tell you every danger spot between here and Cheltenham. Next time you find yourself being waylaid by just such an ancient mariner, blame 'Maus'.

Some guerrilla Mister Toads are also resorting to violent action and destroying the cameras, setting fire to them or spraying their lenses with paint. This terror group even has a name – Mad, or Motorists Against Detection, led by a shadowy figure called 'Captain Gatso' who talks about 'moving into the next phase of our operations'. The *Guardian* reported that one camera on the M11's southbound carriageway in Essex was photographing 2,000 vehicles a day. One day it was found snapped in two, felled, apparently, by a lorry which had reversed against its slender metal stem. Ooopsie. Clumsy me. A camera near Thrapston, Northants, was destroyed by a bomb. Good grief. At this rate Captain Gatso is going to be invited to Downing Street for 'talks about talks'.

Near us there is a speed camera – sited, with typical guile, on a blind corner just yards inside a 30 m.p.h. zone – which seems to be attacked by indignant vandals every other month or so. It takes the roadside grass a few weeks to recover from the scalding. Then it happens again. The cameras do not come cheap, either. They cost around £24,000 a time. Would it not be a better idea to employ a policeman with a clipboard to stand in a location on random days and at unpredictable hours so that motorists would never know when they stood a chance of being caught? Would that not create 'British jobs for British nazis', as Gordon Brown might say, while simultaneously introducing an element of sport to motoring – just the sort of unpredictability which Gatsonides himself used to enjoy when gunning his roadsters down the roads of Europe, grinning away like a mad monkey underneath his oil-spattered driving goggles as he left another Dubonnet mural a-swirl with dust?

Once there was no place for Quislings in Britain but in the age of the Gatso camera any resistance movement must beware interlopers and spies. Motorists Against Detection is opposed by the usual array of goodie goodies and hand wringers who try to infiltrate their ranks and say that, 'Maybe they wouldn't destroy these cameras if they saw the effects of speeding.' But this argument collapses when you consider how many people still do speed. Speed cameras have not stopped speeding. Far from it. All they have done is give habitual snoopers greater power to lift money out of wallets, and for the deranged, professional litter louts of council road-sign departments to clog up our countryside with yet more unwanted signs, this time showing little box-brownie cameras (often a false alarm). Although some areas have seen a drop in road deaths since the introduction of road cameras, others have not, and in Essex in 2003 they actually increased in an area near a camera. In the same year cameras in a group of counties brought in £27 million of fines. What happened to this money? Was it used to improve our schools and hospitals? Don't be silly. That's not the way the inspectorate class works. Only £6 million of the money was sent to the Treasury. The rest was used to buy new cameras.

22 Tony Greig

'Fetch that!' snarls a male, white-South African voice. It is as nasty a sound as the human larynx can make – jagged, guttural, conveying scorn and aggression. It might be the war cry of a Boer pioneer defending his kraal from attacking impis. It might be the scream of a Springbok rugby player charging into a morass of North European forwards, aware that he is about to have the living daylights pummelled out of him.

Such drama! Such violence! The cry of 'Fetch that!' has come, however, from a hunched, gangly man in his late middle age. He is sitting in a commentary box overlooking an English county cricket ground. The setting itself this soft-breezed summer afternoon is bucolic. There is a vista of distant hills, plane trees, slow-moving double-decker buses, all in the lee of a medieval cathedral. A few spectators chew peaceably on soft sandwiches. In the members' enclosure plump women knit and gossip while their husbands doze. The beer tent near the score box is doing slow mid-week morning business, a shandy here, a pale ale there. The mood of the ground is one of contentment, ease with the world, peace.

And yet: 'Fetch that!' The man in the commentary box spits

out the words the moment a batsman hits the third ball of the over for a lovely four. It is a skilful shot, an on-drive that all connoisseurs of cricket would appreciate for its fluency and timing. Even the bowler is able to appreciate the finesse with which it was played, for as he turns on his heels to return to his bowling mark he lets slip a muttered, 'Good shot.' But our commentator is not inclined to dwell on the delicate poetry of the shot. 'That showed 'im. Yeah! Boy, do we have a fight on our hands! Game on!' Snarl, gnarr, grate, yawl. The listener's ear aches at the angularity, the sharpness, not only of the note of the voice but also at the content. Why so bellicose? What's wrong with you, for God's sake? Calm down.

The commentator in question is Tony Greig, one-time captain of the England XI. Greig is not a placid soul. He never has been, probably never will be. And for some reason he feels driven to infect others with his rage and itchy anxiety. He's damned if anyone else is going to be allowed to take life quietly.

Greig is the man who in 1976 sold his services to the Australian broadcasting tycoon Kerry Packer, and in doing so torpedoed the English cricket establishment. In the process he turned a game of manly sportsmanship into a circus of bragging money-grubbers, a circuit where the Aussie dollar meant more than national pride and where the aesthetics of white flannel and good-mannered appeals, of handshakes and intriguing draws, had to be replaced by immediacy and golden rewards, by multi-coloured uniforms, clean-cut results and blaring ground music.

It is in no small part thanks to Greig that English cricket has in recent decades become infected by Australian yappery. The game has become richer, at least in the financial sense. Its top players are now better off than they used to be. But in those same years county cricket has seen its live crowds dwindle. It has lost its soul and sacrificed much of its artistry. It has become just another of the sports which fill the hours on pay-view television, moving wallpaper for the world's sport bars, the action interrupted by star-burst adverts and Greig-style commentators.

Greig was born in South Africa. An all-rounder, he qualified for the England cricket team by dint of a Scottish father and was soon playing for Sussex, where at first they were wowed by the tall, blond outsider. He was never the most sporting of players. His run-out of the West Indies' gentlemanly captain Alvin Kallicharran in 1974 (the last ball of the day had just been bowled and Kallicharran was heading for the pavilion) stirred an enmity which would backfire on Greig. In a later series he vowed to make the West Indies 'grovel'. They duly thrashed England.

Greig always seemed interested by money. He earned many thousands more pounds a year than most of his contemporaries and cashed in with several commercial endorsements, ranging from cricket kit to breakfast cereal. He drove a swanky white Jaguar. He lived in a smart house in Hove. Yet still he wanted more. His God-given talents were not enough. Being captain of England would not suffice. Me, me, me. More, more, more.

In 1977 he signed a deal with an Australian multi-millionaire television tycoon, Kerry Packer. Greig agreed to raise a team of cricketing 'mercenaries' and Greig took some of England's best players with him. Undoubtedly the game had started to neglect its players. Greig's mutiny would never have succeeded if it had not addressed some real resentments. But the furtive deal-making involved and the rampant aggression with which Greig put his case ensured that the split was rancorous. Overnight a game was turned into a business and in the headlong rush much of the dignity of a sporting pursuit was lost. The *raison d'être* of sport, or 'games' as they are better called, is to provide a counter-balance to all life's stresses. When that game itself becomes stressed and ridden with money-making, what is the point of continuing? Why did Tony Greig not just pack his cricket bag and go off to make a fortune in the world of insurance or banking? Perhaps someone could have seized a bag of gold, hit it into the distance with a cricket bat, and cried, 'Fetch that, Greig!'

Cricket has never really recovered. Subsequent England captains have reclaimed a notion of patriotic pride – the idea that they are playing not just for themselves but for their country – but the eyes of the game's national administrators continue to revolve with pound signs. English cricket no longer appears on live terrestrial television because the game has sold its rights to Rupert Murdoch's Greig-scented Sky TV. That decision, incidentally, led to criticism of the Government for allowing big money to rob the public of its cricketing heroes. And the person who voiced that criticism? You guessed it. Tony 'Moneybags' Greig.

23 Edward Heath

Sunday, 21 April 1968, was the moment our country yielded to the sorry creed of multi-culturalism. That evening Edward Heath, leader of the Conservative Party, telephoned Enoch Powell and sacked him from the Shadow Cabinet for making his infamous 'Rivers of Blood' speech about race relations.

'I dismissed Mr Powell because I thought his speech was inflammatory and liable to damage race relations,' said Heath, then a plausible, plummy figure with a high forehead that was almost prototype Cameronian. Heath's fast decision (Powell had given his speech in Birmingham only the previous afternoon) made it almost impossible for British politicians to criticise immigration for the next forty years.

In that vacuum the multi-cultural ideas propagated by the then Home Secretary, Roy Jenkins, went unchallenged. The late Jenkins and his sidekick Anthony Lester (an oily barrister of wearily superior airs who is still up to no good in the House of Lords) may have introduced Britain to multi-culturalism but it was Opposition leader Heath who wielded the more telling influence. By slamming the desktop so hard on Powell's fingers he created a climate of political terror about immigration. The ensuing silence was far more damaging to inter-community relations than old Enoch's mercurial rhetoric.

Heath was a humourless man, a poor public speaker who held the electorate in low esteem. How he won a general election, Lord knows. As he showed with his attitude to Britain's relationship with the European Economic Community (later, and more honestly, the European Union), he thought he knew better than the voters.

At the time of the Powell speech he said he did 'not believe the great majority of the British people share Mr Powell's way of putting his views in his speech'. Note the precision of that claim. Heath was not saying that the great majority of the British people disagreed with Powell about immigration. He was talking about his 'way of putting his views'. It ain't what you say, it's the way that you say it.

Powell had indeed used insulting language – at one point talking about 'charming, wide-grinning picaninnies' following an old white woman down the street and chanting the one word of English they knew, 'racialist'. 'Picaninny' was a lurid, incautious noun and was undeniably racist, but immigration at that time was mainly a black phenomenon. Today it is as much a white affair (from Eastern Europe) and is every bit as open to question. Powell was speaking about the immigration that confronted him and the British people at that time. Powell had also spoken about 'excreta' being pushed through the old woman's letterbox in a multi-racial area. This was probably the more shocking phrase. It coarsened the debate in a way that may have been realistic but was then very shocking to a still polite Britain.

So Heath took umbrage, swiftly. He was leaned on by some members of the Shadow Cabinet to get rid of Powell, a spiky figure who was not prepared to bend to the modernising orthodoxies of the Wilson era. What a smouldering presence he must have been at Shadow Cabinet meetings, declining to join in discussions when he knew he would only disagree with his colleagues. That silence must have driven the less bookish, more emollient politicians in the room mad with uncertainty. Silence can be far more unsettling than an outburst. No wonder some of them wanted him out.

Powell was Shadow Defence Secretary. Did he represent a threat to Heath's leadership? It seems unlikely that such a loner could ever have picked up the support needed for a successful pitch at the party leadership. More persuasive is the suggestion that Heath sacked the man with the penetrating blue gaze and pencil moustache because he, as party leader, needed to assert some machismo. Powell presented a target and had been riding for a swipe. Heath may not have been politically threatened by him but he may have felt intellectually threatened. He rushed into the decision to try to 'kill the story' (hah!) and it could be said that he had a legitimate gripe with Powell for speaking against party policy. Perhaps the Homburg-hatted prophet's worst crime was to voice widespread fears held by the common man, that low-bellied beast from whom the humbly born Heath had done so much to distance himself.

The sacking caused an uproar, bringing Powell's comments

to far wider attention. Dockers and meat traders marched on Parliament to say 'We want Enoch!' Heath's delicate class sensitivities must have been set jangling like a fire engine bell. Race relations were indeed harmed in those early weeks and months, and largely thanks to Heath's over-reaction. How much more effectively he could have defused the situation had he only shown a little wry humour, a wafted 'Enoch will be Enoch' or a tolerant, big-tent 'while I deplore his choice of language it is important that politicians listen to and engage with the fears of their constituents'. But Heath was not that sort of man. He lacked the wit. He lacked the grace. Such qualities matter in a politician. Although high-brows and academics assert that policy is more important than personality, character traits are an essential part of a politician's armoury. They enable him to deal with crises and to manage other politicians. This is every bit as important as policy formation.

Others in British public life looked at what had happened to Powell and, like sheep who have seen a colleague devoured by the wolf, veered away from the danger spot. Immigration became a no-no issue. The only people who could discuss it and claim it for their own were the pro-immigration lobby. When Heath became Prime Minister (the surprise election victory killed Powell's political career) he properly accommodated the Asian refugees from Idi Amin's Uganda but did little to address widespread doubts about immigration. Margaret Thatcher was equally timid when she gained power and under Tony Blair the numbers continued to rise fast. By 2005 we had become a country in which the separation of cultures had fed an ethnic grievance culture which bred British Islamic terrorists. The Thames may not have foamed red but that summer blood from the streets certainly washed into the gutters of London.

Powell had spoken of 50,000 new arrivals a year as being too high. Today the rate is more like 300,000. His language may have been unpleasant but his analysis was pretty much spot on.

Heath went on to prolonged failure. He resented the success of Margaret Thatcher for the last thirty years of his life. It ate away at him, turning him into a squat stewpot of boiling hatred. To see him slumped in his seat below the House of Commons gangway could leave one feeling spiritually dirty, soiled by his unhappiness. How could any human soul sustain such misery over such a long time? There was so much bile in him that it was only a surprise it did not ooze out of the wet corners of his sparsely lashed eyes. It seemed incomprehensible that this bitter man could truly be a pianist and yachtsman. Do musicians not allow the beauty of creation to alleviate their torments? Do sailors not stand in awe of the sea and come to reflect that fate can never be wrestled?

Enoch Powell may have made a racist speech but he was five times the man Edward Heath was.

24 The Very Rev. Ronald Jasper

When York Minster shot up in flames in 1984 there were some who thought the Almighty was exacting revenge. The hetcrodox Bishop of Durham, David Jenkins, had been installed at the Minster a few days earlier. Those flames licking the Minster's roof were divine retribution on Judas Jenkins!

Was it not equally likely that God, morale ground low by the plastic language of modern liturgy, sent down his thunderbolts as a sign of displeasure with another priest, Ronald Jasper? The turbulent Jasper, Dean of York from 1975–84, was the man who more than any other liturgical scholar was responsible for the erosion of the finest expression of religion in the English language, the Book of Common Prayer. For years he badgered archbishops to introduce radical reform of Anglican services. Change, change, change, that was Jasper's goal – and finally he got his way. At his urging the Church produced the Alternative Service Book, the dreaded ASB, unrhythmic, babyish, its prose as tinny as a can of beans. No wonder our churches are nowadays so much more empty. Jasper caused this, the bloody fool.

Certain types of clergy make the mistake of presuming that congregants want to understand and follow every word of what is said at divine service. They delude themselves into thinking that their sermons are a vital part of proceedings. At the altar they pause mid-sentence to lend emphasis to words they feel to be important. They also list special outposts of the Anglican communion – 'we pray today for the Church in Outer Mongolia' – and seriously expect every soul in the pews to bend knee and brow to that particular command.

These priests do not realise, the schmucks, that many churchgoers *feel* prayer rather than thinking it. There are some, probably more than we like to realise, who struggle even to do that. But with time, with repetition of familiar phrases, the soul will respond, albeit in a non-high-brow way. We plug into faith via the singing of hymns or the echo of organ chords or the whiff of incense or the flavour of cold flagstones in our nostrils. Alliteration and metre can lull us into a state of prayerfulness, for instance in the words of the Prayer Book's General Thanksgiving with its 'humble and hearty thanks' and the hope that 'we shew forth thy praise, not only with our lips but in our lives'. Church is an aesthetic experience, a hit to the senses as much as it is a cerebral analysis of what we believe – if indeed we feel certain we believe anything.

The Prayer Book's very age lends it a dignity and a wisdom. We use it (or, until Jasper came along, used it) knowing that generations have gone before us mouthing the same supplications on their journeys from cradle to deathbed. Although we delude ourselves into thinking that today is different and that the twenty-first century poses unmatched challenges, the Book of Common Prayer shows otherwise. Its steady cadences should calm us. Disease, drought, death – all have come and gone in previous centuries. The Prayer Book shows modern mankind that he is not quite so exceptional after all. Far from being elitist, the Prayer Book is fantastically humbling and puts today's Sanhedrin firmly in their place.

Ronald Jasper, alas, did not agree. He devoted himself to tearing down the temple and encouraging the horrid little communion service booklets (of which Series 3 was the worst shocker) which segued into the ASB. Jasper and his cronies ripped the Prayer Book from the hands of a meek Anglican culture. He may not have been quite as violent as Thomas Cromwell during the iconoclastic rampages of the sixteenth century but the result was scarcely less destructive. By the time of his death in 1990 the Church of England was markedly less strong than it had been when he set out on his programme of leeching liturgical diminishment.

Many of the worst disasters to befall Britain in recent years can be traced back to a committee and lo, it came to pass, Ronald Jasper was a great committee man. Committees were where he felt in his element, able to stack votes and build alliances, steer busy chairmen and by-pass flamboyant opponents. The ASB was pretty much written by committee – and reads like it.

In 1963 Jasper pestered Michael Ramsay, then Archbishop of Canterbury, into organising a Joint Liturgical Group. When Ramsay asked who could run such a group he found his eyes being drawn to the nearby figure of Jasper. Oh well, your Grace, if you *insist*. Jasper became the group's secretary. A year later the Archbishop of York, Donald Coggan, decided he wanted to hand over the chairmanship of the Liturgical Commission. Might Jasper, who had pressed hard for the commission to be announced in the first place and had served on it since, be willing to fill in for the Archbishop? Very well, your Grace. Inadequate though I be . . .

Jasper, this latter-day Wolsey, this fiendish combination of radical and self-polished saint, had built himself a reputation as a liturgical expert. That is, he knew about the history of prayers and worship. This made him difficult to beat in scholastic argument. It did not, alas, make him a poet. Nor did it give him a sympathy with the non-intellectual churchgoer, the sort of lay worshipper who looked to matins on Sunday for reassurance and for familiar comfort, a time to blast away at the Te Deum with its two changes of gear, and then to mumble about erring like lost sheep. The trouble with experts is that they know change will bring them work. Without change the expert can find himself short of opportunities to flash his brilliance. Experts very seldom argue for the status quo.

Jasper's commission cleared the ground for the Prayer Book (Alternative and Other Services) Measure of 1965. Soon the Prayer Book was being heaved aside by replacement liturgy. Certainty in worship disappeared. The neophiles were in the cockpit and piloting the aircraft hard – towards misfortune. Three versions of a new liturgy were introduced. Then came the horrid ASB of 1980, reducing worship to the level of inane prattle rather than the haunting beauty of the Prayer Book. By now hundreds of thousands of hours of time had been spent by clergymen and lay volunteers on committee discussion, time which might have been better spent engaged in ministry or simple church maintenance. The impression given was of a Church consumed with its own affairs and which lacked faith in its past. No wonder the flock fled.

The ASB did not last. In fact it was almost farcically short-lived and today it may not be used in authorised services, having been replaced by an even newer bit of nonsense, Common Worship. But the damage has been done. Anglicans returning to church worship in their middle years, as has always been the pattern, find nothing familiar on which to lean. The history and the wonderment have been removed from many services, like outer layers of paint being stripped from a great oil painting by over-enthusiastic restorers. Although Cranmer's masterpiece has made a modest return in some parishes, others continue to be haunted by the ghost of the vandalistic Ronald Jasper. Knowledge of the Prayer Book is now so limited that when Prince Charles and Camilla Parker-Bowles used its general Confession for their wedding blessing some newspaper editors seized on its words – 'our manifold sins and wickedness . . . provoking most justly thy wrath and indignation . . . we are heartily sorry for these our misdoings; the remembrance of them is grievous unto us' – as an extraordinary admission of adultery. These editors had no idea that such words were historic acknowledgements of humanity and its flaws. Perhaps morning conference on Fleet Street should occasionally begin with that Confession.

As churchgoers we are taught to forgive those who sin against us. Looking at the forlorn ruin that is currently the Church of England it is hard to summon much in the way of forgiveness for Ronald Jasper. May he rest in peace, however, the stupid, unyielding, tradition-trashing fool. And may we never forget the lessons of his terrible misdoings.

25 Graham Kelly

Not many multi-billion-pound businesses owe their existence to a myopic, mumbling former Blackpool bank teller, but that is the case with English football's Premier League. Big-time soccer, with its flash cars, trashy values, vast pay-offs, dodgy foreign money, twisted finances and scavenging agents – in short, one of the unchecked fountains of decadence in Britain today, gushing raw greed into society's open gutters – would not be what it is today but for the efforts of a gormless football administrator called Graham Kelly.

Two decades ago this Kelly, rotund and bespectacled, was the public face of the 'beautiful game'. On the pitch it may have offered bronzed, muscular Adonises. Off the pitch it gave us the inadequate Kelly, a prize specimen of the genus *football administratus incompetus*. Somehow or other – there must have been a lamentable shortage of candidates – he had become chief executive of the Football Association in 1988. His tenure saw football reach a low ebb. This may have been coincidence or the two may have been directly linked.

The FA runs the game in England, both at the wide amateur level (the Hackney Marshes leagues and their counterparts across the country) and also the narrower professional game. The FA should be feared and respected in equal measure, rather like a good referee. It has the power to expel any club which misbehaves or breaks its codes. Expulsion could put a club out of business but things should never reach that stage.

In addition to running Wembley stadium and the FA Cup the Association guards the soul of football, looks after its rules, manages disciplinary matters and tries to ensure that the English national team wins a few games. Such were the burdens which faced chief executive Kelly, a grammar school boy from Poulton-le-Fylde who started his working life behind the counter at Barclays Bank.

There is, alas, a huge gap between weighing bags of sixpences for Mr Arkwright the greengrocer of a Friday afternoon and sitting down with some of the sharpest sheepskin coats in the Western world to negotiate valuable TV rights for professional football. This gap proved to be one that Robert Henry Graham Kelly was unable to bridge. Before that chasm became undeniably clear, alas, Kelly allowed the richest clubs in the land to set up a breakaway league and take their TV rights with them.

The FA colluded in the formation of the Premier League because it hoped it might nurture some better England players and, it is said, for the petty political reason that it would muck up the old Football League (a rival of the FA). The second may have happened but the first most certainly has not. The Premier League has gone on a mad foreign spending spree and some of our top football clubs now have few England-qualified players. At the same time the distribution of TV money throughout the professional game has withered. The split used to be 50 per cent to the First Division, 25 per cent to the Second Division, and 25 per cent between the Third and Fourth Divisions. Now the split is 91 per cent (of some £2.7 billion) to the Premier League with the other scrapings being shared among the rest.

Should we care? Is this not an example of strong businesses reaping their due? Reap they most certainly have. The directors and managers and star players and coaches and players' agents all make enormous sums of money out of the game. But the idea of football as a game, as a pleasurable activity, as a diversion from life's more serious demands, has been lost. A Second Division football club can give its town or city a strong sense of identity and comradeship. If run well, and if it has the money, it can enthuse local boys and get them to do some exercise rather than loaf around the streets in the evenings. A local football team can provide local heroes, pin-ups whose behaviour can help set an example. But if that local football team is going bust, thanks to a rotten deal signed by the Football Association, such admirable things will not happen.

This is what happened in 1992 when Kelly and his FA colleagues signed away the TV rights to top football. Money which would have gone to the provinces and to the lower-ranked teams of English football went instead to pampered international stars, allowing them to buy another Maserati for the garage, another mistress for the penthouse, another raucous night out in the city centre where reprobate behaviour will generate misery and from which all sense of civic respect is absent.

This is the amoral, venal, shallow world which Graham Kelly's disastrous 1992 deal with the Premier League created. Kelly was about as far from an ideal public face for football as could be imagined. He was unfit. He spoke in a wheezy, high-pitched voice. On television, when being grilled under the studio lights, he would regularly push his glasses up his sweaty nose. He had no natural command or wit. He may have made the likes of Beckham and Owen and Drogba unbelievably rich. But he rendered the rest of us a great deal poorer.

26 Graham Kendrick

One of the more excruciating dilemmas in twenty-first-century Britain – makes your toes curl like Ali Baba's slippers – is attending a wedding or christening and discovering that your friends have chosen a happy-clappy hymn. How could they?

The organ strikes up some plinkety-plop notes, saccharine chords which sound like something off a bad Disney film. There follows a syncopated chorus and inane words ascribed to someone maybe called 'Bob' or 'Brian', well-meaning but prosaic mooncalves who have presumed to oust the genius of Wesley and Bach. 'And now, from the *BBC Songs of Praise* book, number 231, "If I were a Butterfly"', simpers the priest. His weak smile lends him the air of a ruminant with gaseous afflictions. Up strikes the tune, feeble-minded, numbingly repetitive. That particular masterpiece about the butterfly contains the lines,

> And if I were a fuzzy wuzzy bear,
> I'd thank you, Lord, for my fuzzy wuzzy hair
> But I just thank you, Father, for making me me.

Corporal Jones from *Dad's Army* would be in his element. Fuzzy wuzzies, indeed. So there you stand in the pews, appalled, mutinous. Do you refuse to sing a note? Or do you mumble along in the choral equivalent of a dirty protest and as the last notes fade utter a stage whisper to your wife, saying, 'What a perfectly *ghastly* hymn'? You certainly, if you have any self-respect, give a barrel or two to the priest as you leave the church. Protest to the clerics is important. We shouldn't let them get away lightly with this drivel.

Happy-crappy hymns are a pestilence. They demean adult worship, dragging it to a level even lower than that of Mrs C.F. Alexander's 'All Things Bright and Beautiful' (1848). They are self-obsessed, babyish, clichéd, simplistic. They try not to use too many multi-syllable words lest the poor lambs in the church become confused. No 'consubstantial, co-eternal' as in the seventh-century 'Blessed City Heavenly Salem' here, thank you. The butterfly song even has accompanying actions. When they get to the fuzzy wuzzy line they froth up their hair and, for all I know, do black and white minstrel-style smiles.

Several authors have written these appalling hymns. In the case of the fuzzy wuzzies it was someone called Brian Howard, a guitar-strumming 'humorist' whose other contribution to the historic canon of Western ecclesiastical music is a hymn 'I Just Wanna be a Sheep'. You don't have long to scramble for safety with that one before it has you mouthing the words 'I pray the Lord my soul to keep, I just wanna be a sheep, Baa baa, baa, baa'.

The daddy of them all when it comes to such gloopy nonsense, however, is Graham Kendrick, author of 'Shine, Jesus, Shine'. If they ever do an accompanying video it will no doubt portray Christ as a window cleaner on his ladder. Kendrick, who has a personal website complete with a briskly efficient shopping section, is the nation's pre-eminent churner-outer of evangelical bilge. This man is the king of happy-clappy banalities. He started writing hymns in the late 1960s (age of flower-power gormlessness) and has now written 400 of the ruddy things. Quantity, as ever, has thrived at the expense of quality.

The jazzy chorus of 'Shine, Jesus, Shine' is particular agony, accompanied, as it often is, by a couple of show-offs in the front pews raising their arms and swinging them from side to side. The hand-gesture brigade do not let themselves be deterred by the minor detail of holding a hymn book at the same time. Such is their Messianic zeal that they learn the lines off by heart, the better to gyrate and lean. 'Oh, come on, it's only a hymn,' the appeasers say. But it is much more than that. It is a fight for English culture.

Familiar old hymns are being ripped away like ivy. *Hymns Ancient and Modern*, full of muscular harmonies, is being dumped from parish churches as the happy-clappy plague spreads. The green cloth covers of the *English Hymnal*, filled with Ralph Vaughan Williams's adaptations of medieval English airs, are now rarely seen.

It will not be long before a happy-clappy hymn is played at a coronation. It's little short of a miracle that King's College, Cambridge, has not been forced to accommodate the syncopation tendency in its annual Christmas carol service.

Traditionalists elsewhere are being forced to yield and 'accept that times have moved on'. Should it not be a strength of Anglican worship that it does *not* move with the times and instead provides continuity at a time of baffling change? But it seems we must always cede to toothpaste-scented freaks with razored beards and plodding chord sequences. Out with the harmonium! In with the electric guitar! Out with the hymns sung by our forebears, such as 'He Who Would Valiant Be' and 'Hills of the North'. In with some soupy Daniel O'Donnell hit or the roughage-rich 'Bind Us Together' or the negro spiritual cum grammatical solecism 'It is Me, Me, O Lord'.

The hero of these neophiles, this Kendrick, is a lazy writer. Imagine Pam Ayres without the humour. There is little variety in his rhythms and he trots out some frightful old chestnuts. He calls religious love 'pure as the whitest snow'. Come on, man, even a schoolgirl would blush to use that one again. Hands are always being held in his hymns. 'Different faces' is followed, inevitably, by 'different races'. Joy comes in rivers. So do grace and mercy. Graham is fond of a river. Such a powerful metaphor, innit?

Just when congregations may be trying to raise their souls to higher things, Kendrick slips a mention of traffic jams into his hymn 'Wish I Could Cry (Another Bad Day at the World)'. One minute you are trying to envisage the Holy Ghost. The next minute an image of a Mini Metro is thrust at you.

Sometimes Kendrick does not even bother to maintain his simplistic rhymes. In 'You're the Perfume, I'm the Jar' the aa, bb scheme breaks down in the penultimate verse. The last word of that song (Kendrick and his lot dislike the word 'hymn') is 'Ah'. 'Urrrgh' might have been more accurate. My sister-in-law, whose parish church in Derbyshire has been colonised by happy clappies, reports that there is another go-ahead hymn which has a Cossack flavour and ends in the word 'hoi!' Good grief. 'Oh, but the children love these songs,' say defenders. No they don't. When a happy-clappy hymn is chosen at my children's school chapel rehearsals a shout goes up from scores of voices: 'It's one of the crappy modern jobs!'

While church attendance figures continue to go gurgling down the drain, supporters of these new hymns argue that there is 'nothing wrong in being happy'. Nothing wrong in it, agreed. But not all congregants want to, or are able to, radiate happiness all the time. One of the characteristics of English Protestantism is its discretion and the privacy it allows the worshipper. This has been moulded by our North European reserve. It suits the native English character. There may be a time and place for happiness but church worship is a time for inner examination, not bullying, incessant gaiety. People often come to church at times of crisis in their lives, be it death or family pressure, career difficulty or spiritual anxiety. They may be in a fragile state. And yet here are the happy clappies insisting that they bang a tambourine, just as they insist that the inner spell of adult supplication be ruptured in their communion services in order to shake hands or kiss neighbours at the 'sign of peace'.

The sturdy hymns of England, musical embodiment of the stoicism, resolve and undemonstrative solidarity of our nation, are in severe peril, and all thanks to ill-shaven remnants of the late 1960s, grinning inadequates who have never got over the fact that they weren't Cat Stevens. Our church music is being eroded by the pulverisingly puerile. Say a prayer for it. But please, whatever you do, don't burst into the butterfly song.

27 Sir Denys Lasdun

During the twentieth century Western architecture underwent a moral breakdown when popular ideas of beauty were treated with contempt. Buildings were imposed on the public, often by government officials, rather as sour medicine is thrust down the throat of a reluctant child. What occurred in Britain was arguably even worse than what happened in old Eastern Bloc countries such as Romania (where Ceausescu destroyed much of old Bucharest) because it was the work of a small clique of 'experts' and public servants rather than one crazed dictator.

The brutalism which wrecked many English town centres in the 1950s and 1960s was a widespread deceit, selfish radicalism being passed off as superior knowledge. The best, or rather worst, example of brutalist architecture is London's National Theatre. It should in fact be called the Royal National Theatre but the people who run it (thanks to generous public subsidy) do not like to use the 'Royal'. They find monarchy a distasteful concept. It has popular support, you see. They can't be doing with such vulgarities.

Denys Lasdun was the go-ahead architect, a disciple of Le

Corbusier and of intellectual modernism, who in 1963 managed to win the contract to design the theatre. The insides of the theatre, by and large, are blameless – although the carpet has a strange habit of giving you electric shocks if you use the metal banisters on the stairs. The openness of the entrance area, with its nightly pre-show concerts, is certainly more successful than the cramped foyers of many of Shaftesbury Avenue's commercial theatres, those creaking show palaces of the Victorian era.

The act of vandalism, of intellectual arrogance, came with the exterior of the theatre's huge building. It was not only built out of a disgusting grey reinforced concrete but was also shaped like a series of pill boxes stacked on top of each other. Lasdun's preferred term for this was 'strata'. He claimed they owed something to the strata found in certain forms of geology. It is hard to believe, however, that Mother Nature could ever devise something quite as hideous as the strata of the Royal National Theatre.

On completing his drawings did Lasdun lean back in his chair and say to himself, 'Yes, that looks really beautiful. That will give theatregoers a sense of wonder. That will seize the imagination of passers-by and persuade them to step inside this temple of dreams'? Or did he strike the desk with self-justification, delighted to have produced a design which so quickly summed up his philosophy that the little people and their petty-bourgeois tastes counted for nothing beside the high-brow thinkers of modernist architecture?

Some said, 'Give it time – the shock will pass and it will eventually become a much-loved part of the London skyline.'

Well, it has not happened yet. The external ungainliness of Lasdun's 'masterpiece' has yet to find much public favour forty-five years on from its conception. The National sits there on the South Bank, somehow both squat and offensively big, a grey blot on the sweeping Thames's flank. The theatre's managers seem to realise that the concrete exterior is foul to the eye. Recently they allowed installation artists to coat the theatre's horribly grey fly tower in grass for a few days. The green turf looked very much better than that rain-streaked, rough-surfaced concrete. Lasdun argued that the finish of the concrete made it look 'archaic'. Balls. It simply looks as though it has been scraped by the bucket forks of a JCB digger.

Like many modern architects Lasdun talked a good game. He was a skilful schmoozer, boastful in a nicely high-falutin' way. 'Architecture, for me at any rate,' he murmured, 'only makes sense as the promoter and extender of human relations.' What prize bullshit from the creator of such a right-angled, inhuman monstrosity. His politics were in keeping with the time: off-the-peg London liberal, buying into all that guff about architecture's 'empowerment' and 'social commitment'. Why is it that people who profess to have the greatest regard for the working classes are so contemptuous of their tastes? *Bien pensants* adored Lasdun. It was the 'lower orders' who were baffled and appalled. Plus the Prince of Wales. God bless him, the Prince saw right through the waffle and said that Lasdun's effort was 'a clever way of building a nuclear power station in the middle of London without anyone objecting'.

The Royal National Theatre was not Lasdun's only rotten

memento to the nation. He was also responsible for 'cluster' blocks of flats – as many as four sharing the same lift core block. They were not popular. He came up with the University of East Anglia, a building whose occupants have had to learn to live with leaks and difficult temperatures. Lasdun, aware of the power of a soundbite, said that the campus would assume the feel of a 'landlocked harbour'. Given its leaks, it was probably just as well there was no real harbour.

The University of London commissioned Lasdun and in the process wrecked a Georgian area of the capital. Poor old Christ's College, Cambridge, also bought it: a block very similar to East Anglia (same graph paper, perhaps – nothing like flogging an old idea). It has not been wildly popular and is horribly unsympathetic to its neighbouring buildings.

Lasdun, not short of self-esteem, was apoplectic when people tried to alter his buildings – or even, quite understandably, suggested setting about them with the demolisher's ball and crane. A shop in the Strand was flattened, giving Lasdun a frightful attack of the vapours. A block of Lasdun flats in Bethnal Green came close to being pulled down, but it survived for the time being and the architect's defenders now point out that the flats change hands for huge sums. How socialist is that?

It is for wrecking London's artistic quarter of the Thames's South Bank, however, and for posing as a grandee of reinforced concrete to a generation of younger architects, that Lasdun deserves his raspberry. A reinforced raspberry.

28 Dame Suzi Leather

Public modesty is no longer thought necessary in our ruling
elite. Take a recent issue of *Charity Commission News*. In
the past this would have been a worthy journal offering sober
advice and presenting news items with the objectivity once
thought essential in state organisations. Its very dullness would
have been a virtue, a reassurance, a sign that the Charity
Commission was not some house of passing fads but a cold,
stolid pillar of the body politic, cautious, measured.

Issue number 27 of *Charity Commission News*, published at
the start of 2008, was of a different character. Its front page
was devoted to a jaunty message from the commission's 'chair',
Dame Suzi Leather, complete with a facsimile of her signature
(the modern handwriting round yet standy-uppy, shouting:
'I'm capable, I'm confident'). The tone of Madam Chair's
message was patronising, saying how a recent holiday had
surely left everyone with 'recharged batteries' and eager to press
on with their plans for the 'exceptionally busy' times ahead.
Charity workers who happened to be suffering from depression
or wasting illness must have been left perplexed and insulted
by such schoolmarmy insistence on the upbeat.

Leather's message then turned to some positive spin about controversial new charities legislation passed by the Labour Government – legislation which some people in the charity world had opposed bitterly. These new laws, said Dame Suzi airily, offered charities 'greater flexibility and control'. The matter could be better understood if readers acquired some booklet about 'The Office of the Third Sector'. Having thus dispensed the latest apparatchik cliché and spread New Labour's word to her adoring flock, Dame Suzi signed off with a regal, 'I wish you all a very successful year'. Quite the Lady Muck!

Dame Suzi Leather has form. Pushy and politically driven, she is known as the 'Queen of the Quangocrats' for her record of taking prominent public jobs and stepping in front of the TV cameras at frequent opportunities. As a feminist she cannot be content for her physical attributes (fresh face, lean limbs, boyish hairdo) to be used to assert her political persona. She may be a hard-boiled state meddler and off-the-peg leftwinger but the fact she is photogenic and looks like a private school yummy-mummy guarantees her oodles of publicity – and that brings her power. What a pity that her appearance on *Any Questions* at the start of this year laid bare a dour lack of humour. Image over content, that's our gal.

Educated privately at the wildly posh St Mary's, Calne, and later at Exeter and Leicester universities, where she read social work and politics, Leather started adult life in 1979 as a researcher for a consumer-rights outfit. I say 'Leather', but her married surname is now Hampsher-Monk. Her double-barrelled husband is a professor.

In the 1980s Comrade Suzi become a trainee probation officer and then a freelance consumer consultant, whatever that is (professional busybody, I think). Having paused momentarily in her endeavours to pop out three children she became 'chair' of the Exeter and District National Health Service Trust before turning her attentions to the new growth sector of food nannyism. Mad cow disease had given the Left the opportunity it craved to impose greater control of agriculture and food production. It did this under the cover of consumer protection. She duly became No. 2 at the Food Standards Agency, newly created by the Blair Government. This was seen in some quarters as a reward for criticisms she had made of Nicholas Soames MP when he was the Tories' food minister.

Public servants once went to great lengths to keep their political loyalties out of the news. They were supposedly impartial dispensers of government in the public cause, not activists for a particular party. Dame Suzi does not trifle with such a pretence, however. She smiles indulgently when it is said that she is a Labour voter and a Christian Socialist. Thus continues the casual politicisation of our civil service and its counterparts in quango world, a trend which has so reduced public trust in our institutions and enfeebled our state.

In 2002 leftwing Suzi gobbled down a big one: she was given the job of chairing the Human Fertilisation and Embryology Authority. Boy, what a meal. It was like seeing a frog wait for hours on the river bank before copping an enormous dragonfly. Gulp. Gotcha, baby. Chew, chew, chew. Burrrrrrp.

She became a regular fixture on television news, producers

being pathetically grateful to use her slender physique in stories which might otherwise feature nothing but test tubes and scientists in white coats. Dame Suzi became quite the poster girl for modern, Blairite attitudes. She exemplified the liberal posh middle classes, the we-know-better brigade, the crowd who are intent on running petty aspects of our lives, even when we are quite happy running them ourselves, while simultaneously loosening the law's moral restraints. Her regime thrust ever onwards in the name of 'appropriate' attitudes and modernity. During her time in control the authority decided that it was in order for women with breast cancer genes to have their embryos tested to weed out ones which might have an undesirable gene. A step towards eugenics? Dame Suzi's plausible media manner soon quelled any such criticism. This was about women's health, thank you. In other controversies – she's a great one for a controversy, which brings yet more publicity – she said that she saw no need for fathers in IVF families. To think a child should have both a male and female parent was 'old-fashioned'. Pouff! Just like that, common sense was dismissed.

Although she was still comparatively new to public life she became a dame in January 2006, Blair's Downing Street being hopelessly in love with her image. Later that year she took over at the Charity Commission, a slightly cobwebbed, decent organisation which quietly got on with its work and made life difficult for nobody. Enter Dame Suzi. She fell into step with government thinking which wanted to attack private schools. Even though she herself uses private schooling she hungrily set about reforms of the way the Commission views public schools. There was talk of spot checks being made to ensure that public schools do their bit for the wider community. Unless they can show how 'accessible' they are being to the poor they will lose their charitable status, and with it the right to claim back some tax.

Until this point there had been a principle that education, in itself, was a charitable activity. After all, it trains our future teachers and doctors and scientists. Without the excellence of public school graduates, Britain would be immeasurably less competent. Yes, but private schools do something inexcusable, too. They show up the standards in our state schools. In the 1960s there was little difference between state grammars and public schools. Now, after five decades of political interference, the gap is wide and expanding. The state-control fanatics are furious. Dame Suzi Leather is doing their dirty work, even though she will probably drive many schools to give up their charitable status, and thus make private education even less affordable.

Leather was once asked what she made of the sobriquet 'Quango Queen'. She replied coldly that she did 'not know what it meant'. Let us help you, Suzi. 'Quango Queen' means 'unelected harridan who draws her money from the public sector and sticks her nose into other people's business, making their lives considerably less easy'. The only consolation is the thought that if the Tories manage to win the next general election she will be out on her ear before you can say 'Hampsher-Monk'.

29 John McEnroe

Any young games player today soon learns the ways of modern Britain: the referee's word may well not be final. This is also true of the umpire, the touch-judge, the linesman and other sports officials. It is true of other fields of endeavour, be it the exam marker or the prize adjudicator, the local government inspector or the middle-ranking magistrate. All can be questioned and fairly easily slandered. The referee's decision, far from being final, is merely one stage in a potentially long process of complaints, appeals and lawyerly whingeing with which the determined plaintiff can pursue a goal of defiant self-assertion long after the heat of the battle.

This widespread undermining of the referee (and other official authority figures) as a fount of impartiality can be traced back to an afternoon at the Wimbledon tennis championships in 1981. That may not have been the first time it happened, but for the British it was one of the first times we noticed it. It was the first time many of us saw it on telly, and therefore the first time we believed it.

A young American player lost his temper with the umpire. A call had gone against the American and he refused to accept

it without a fight. 'Man,' he screamed, 'you cannot be serious.' Rant, rant, rant. Pout of lip. 'Man.' Ugh.

Until that point few tennis players had been seen talking to an umpire, let along shouting at one. The most we had seen was Ilie Nastase, so Romanian and romantic that he did not really count. Excitable Latins you expected to behave this way. But not Americans.

John McEnroe, the American in question, was one of the most skilful tennis players not only of his era but probably of all time. He was prey, however, to displays of such childish peevishness that he cannot properly claim to be a 'sporting great'. No one who shrieks at low-paid officials, 'You guys are the pits of the world, you know that?' can rightly be called a 'great', unless 'great pain in the backside' is intended. Anyway, McEnroe was not good-looking. He was not from a poor family. He was just a rich kid from the United States, spouting anger and a well-honed sense of his own entitlement.

McEnroe helped to spread bad sportmanship to a generation of youngsters. They saw how his tantrums won him fortune and notoriety, observed how his cross little outbursts could unsettle his opponents, and took note of the way they simultaneously seemed to help McEnroe 'pump himself up'. They duly started to wheedle in a similar fashion. At the same time the theory went round that it was somehow good to be aggressive because that was how you could win. (The theory was flawed, for McEnroe lost a celebrated Wimbledon final to the outwardly phlegmatic Bjorn Borg.) McEnroe's nasty habits were also taken as being intrinsically American. The good work of scores of American philanthropists in creating a favourable impression of US values was undone by this bad loser in the sweat band and gym shoes.

McEnroe's on-court misbehaviour was in keeping with his background. His father was a New York lawyer. No further questions, your honour! New York lawyers seldom got where they are today by being polite souls who meekly accept the rulings of their superiors. New York lawyers are people for whom the words 'awkward' and 'sods' might well have been invented. McEnroe's father was not a particularly niggly specimen of the breed so far as I know but he was a New York lawyer all the same. Nuff said.

What a bad loser his son was. He often burst into tears. He thwopped his racquet on the ground or on the steps of the umpire's elevated seat. He threw his towel away in disgust. He huffed and puffed and glowered at the middle distance. All because he was not winning a mere game of tennis. Some tried to depict his behaviour as the righteous anger of a poor boy striving to overcome the hurdles placed in his way by a snobbish tennis 'establishment', but it is hard to see a lawyer's son from New York – a city run for lawyers by lawyers, to the general detriment of the rest of the globe – as a waif. McEnroe's filthy manners may have had more to do with a nose for controversy and the awareness that every time he abused an umpire he would increase his value as a marketing tool.

A man gripped by the simple and laudable desire to perform at his best, you say. Your acceptance of his motives does you credit but does not carry the day. Before McEnroe lost his temper he was good to watch. When he threw a tantrum he was in some ways even better to watch. He surely knew this. He went on to repeat that 'you cannot be serious' line several times. Television schedulers were duly grateful and McEnroe continues to be employed, for handsome rewards, as a TV commentator.

We hear little from Bjorn Borg these days. McEnroe, on the other hand, is rarely silent. 'Twas ever thus.

30 Stephen Marks

One of the most miserable, shaming, dog-dirt-nasty things about Britain today is the coarseness of language in public. Four-letter swear words are not just common but *de rigueur*. Among the under-thirties in particular foul language flows unthinkingly, blurted out, sicked forth, one long projectile spurt of obscenity, spouted in me-too fashion.

They do not particularly mean it. The profanities drift out of these mouths like gaseous green bile, rising to fill the void. These dullards do not notice how unpleasant they are being. Swearing has become endemic in both men and women, across all classes, faiths and regions.

As recently as ten years ago it was fun to take a child for a ride on the top deck of a London bus. Today that is no treat. The language bandied about is now so flecked by F words and C words and all manner of X words, ejaculated, barked, yelped with casual abandon, that you might as easily be in the trench on the Western Front during an enemy shell barrage. During battles men at least have good reason for sulphurous exclamations. The same cannot be said of wealthy, twenty-first-century Britain:

so much vituperation, so much sloppy profanity, provoked by such . . . comfort.

What has this vile state of affairs got to do with a little-known, sixty-year-old clothes retailer called Stephen Marks? Well, rather a lot. This man Marks, possibly amoral, possibly worse than that, has encouraged a generation of Britons to think lightly about foul language – indeed, to treat it as a joke. Stephen Marks is the man who literally 'f***ed up' Britain.

He has certainly made the money. In 1969 Marks set himself up in business under the title French Connection. The name 'French Connection' first belonged to a drug-trafficking scheme between Turkey and Marseille, France. It was not a glamorous operation. Its operators included Corsican mafiosi with links to the Second World War's Gestapo. Tasteful.

Quite why Marks felt this was a name worth giving to his fledgling fashion house we can only guess. Did he consider drugs – or even maybe the Gestapo – to be attractive? Was this an early example of 'heroin chic'?

French Connection received a boost early in its life when Hollywood made a film of that name. It starred Gene Hackman as a New York policeman called Jimmy 'Popeye' Doyle, had one of the great car chases of movie history and took the Oscar for best film of 1971. Marks must have congratulated himself on his cleverness in choosing so catchy a name. If only 20th Century-Fox had made a film called 'Grace Brothers', Mrs Slocombe and Co. could have become retailing giants.

During the 1970s and 1980s French Connection – and the egregious Marks – prospered in a steady but quiet way, selling

clothes for children and grown-ups. It was in 1997 that Marks
hit the big time. A fax arrived in his office intended for his
Hong Kong department. The fax contained a typing mistake.
Instead of referring to FCHK (French Connection Hong Kong)
it said FCUK. Marks saw this and thought it a great idea. An
advertising campaign was born.

The campaign used the anagram – sorry, acronym – in
lower-case letters, the better to nudge the eye into 'getting' the
'joke'. French Connection clothes now carried these letters
prominently, often on the outside of the garment. Packaging,
coat hangers, shop fronts – everything was altered to proclaim
'fcuk'. There was nothing subtle about this campaign. Marks
decorated his Oxford Street shop with a banner saying 'the
world's biggest fcuk'.

Oh, how a nation laughed. Well, for about five minutes. After
that the result of Marks's money-grabbing initiative (his profits
trebled) was more corrosive. Children were confronted by the
letters and presumed it must be all right to be suggestive and
brassy and foul-mouthed. 'Sub-brands' were created with slogans
such as 'fcuk at home', 'fcuk spirit' and 'fcuk spa'. The campaign
soon reached America – against the better judgement of a few
voices such as New York's Mayor Rudi Giuliani – and
advertisements included a sexual clinch between a man and
woman which ended with a picture of a condom bearing the
fcuk logo. All this, please, to flog a few heavily marked-up
clothes.

Not content with having cheapened public discourse Marks
has taken it upon himself to sue small organisations with similar

initials in their names. A computer called First Consultant UK found itself accused of trademark infringement. Young Conservative Party members who tried a lighthearted stunt with Conservative Future UK were also given a legal monstering.

The fashion business often boasts that it is socially responsible. Indeed, Mark and his cronies make high-tone claims about reducing their 'impact on the environment'. This environment does not seem to embrace the notion of visual and moral pollution by the puerile endorsement of bad language.

There are signs of a fight-back. In 2003 a judge in Mold Crown Court dismissed a juror who was wearing an fcuk t-shirt. 'The misspelling of a basic Anglo-Saxon word on a garment hardly dignifies the court proceedings,' he said. 'It is beyond me why anyone can think they should wear anything like that in public, particularly in a court.'

Those of us who take this view are dismissed as fogeys. But is it really so fogeyish to wish to live in a world where you are not assailed by bad language at every turn? Is bad language not often a precursor of other forms of anti-social and violent behaviour? If we do not protest about bad language what hope have we of stopping thuggery and vandalism?

Thank God King Cnut never thought of going into the rag trade.

31 Michael Martin

There is not much point in having a House of Commons if it is not fairly run. If there is not much point in having a House of Commons there is even less point having a Parliament, amusing and quirky though the House of Lords can be. And if there is not much point in having a Parliament there is no point having elected representatives – in short, a democracy. We might as well have the country run instead by an American businessman, or a Swiss bank, or the head of the Armed Forces, as happens in some perfectly prosperous corners of Asia.

A military dictatorship is not entirely without its attractions. It would be cheaper. The buses would run on time. The settled view of the British people at present, however, seems to be that we will stick with our untidy democracy.

The Speaker of the House of Commons is therefore an important figure. He or she has the task of ensuring that discussions in the Chamber of the Commons are properly supervised, there being no bias against certain MPs simply on account of their accents or their backgrounds or their political philosophies. Barring perhaps a minor favour here and there to the elderly, the infirm and the dotty, Members should be equal. If that brick of equality

is missing then, as we have seen, the entire edifice of parliamentary democracy is imperilled. It is not the responsibility of the Speaker to decide what is debated and at what time. That is organised by the various party Whips, sometimes known as 'the usual channels'. Nor must the Speaker, oddly enough, make parliamentary speeches. 'Speaker' is an unsatisfactory name but we are stuck with it.

For the past eight years we have also been stuck with Michael Martin as our Speaker. He has been an exceptionally bad one and his tenure has weakened the office and weakened our public life.

The Speaker has a major hand in selecting which Hon. Members get to speak – and, more important, of ensuring that they can be heard. This is how the vast apparat of modern government comes to be questioned. This is how ministerial decisions are examined, supposedly without fear or favour. Mr Martin has failed to encourage this as he should. Under his Speakership the Government has got away with murder.

Mr Martin is a former Labour MP. One says 'former' because, on becoming Speaker, he was obliged automatically to relinquish ties to the party machine which brought him to Westminster from working-class beginnings in Glasgow. Ideally a Speaker should, like a good high court judge, appear to be an almost other-worldly figure. He or she should certainly not parade too much personal history, for that might be to betray political leanings. Speakers must be impartial. When it comes to party politics, or to concepts of left or right, they should be as opaque as the glass in a municipal lavatory. That is essential to be trusted as a fair arbiter.

Michael Martin, alas, has been a disaster in this respect. He has worn his upbringing heavily on the sleeves of his Speaker's robes. He often refers to his past career as a metal basher. He actively projects an image of himself as a working-class boy made good. He boasts about his days as a trade union negotiator. 'Friends' of this Speaker brief the press about how good it is to have a class warrior in such a position.

If this does not shout 'Labour', Martin's crassness as a match referee during noisy Commons confrontations has led Opposition MPs (and some on the Government side) to conclude that he is not even-handed in his rulings. Repeatedly he has been open to accusations of favouring Labour MPs (particularly Scottish men) over Conservatives (particularly those with fruity accents). Sitting in his large Chair, Speaker Martin has not been a distant figure in wig and tights, as he might have been. He has declined to wear ceremonial garb and has happily leaned over the side of his Chair to chat to old Labour lags.

He does not have a quick mind. All right, let's be blunt. He's as thick as cold custard. He has more than once lost his temper, jabbing a finger and spitting fury at an aristocratic Tory, at other times turning bright red in the face while screaming as order. Away from the Chamber he has resorted to hiring, as his spokesman, one of London's most notorious libel lawyers.

'Mick' Martin, far from being a credit to the House, has been a clumsy class warrior, a figure of lamentable comedy, a Speaker who does not enjoy the trust and esteem which is essential to his important office. It may be no coincidence that his tenure has coincided with a time of low public standing for Parliament and politicians. With this gallumphing idiot as Speaker, is it any wonder the House of Commons is regarded as a joke?

32 Alun Michael

One Saturday morning last November I took my two daughters, aged nine and four, to a hunt meet. All seemed rosy at first but it soon became apparent that cold, crisp West Country morning how wickedly twisted our nation's values have become – and all thanks to a stupid law created by a dismal little doormat called Alun Michael.

Fox hunting, as traditionally practised, became an illegal activity during Tony Blair's second term. Hundreds of hours of parliamentary effort were devoted to its extermination. MPs bent over backwards to criminalise an outdoor sport pursued by some of the most upstanding members of the community.

Pro-hunt activists at one point invaded the Commons Chamber, leading to rewardingly farcical scenes as rangy kennel men and hunt bloods from the shires ran rings round portly parliamentarians. The hunt lads were eventually collared by the tailcoated doormen, but since that day they have, in a different way, continued to make the Westminster crowd look stupid.

The Government minister who pushed through the hunting ban was Alun Michael. To look at he is not a striking proposition, a careworn creature with the hunched shoulders and lank hair of a natural loser. He has a pallid, cheerless complexion. His voice is unexceptional. His suits are neither too smart nor too dowdy. Alun Michael is an authentic middler, a worker bee, putty in the hands of more confident colleagues. This was not the first dirty job he had been handed by Tony Blair. He was also made First Minister of Wales when Blair needed a placeman. He did not last long.

On the hunting ban Michael was not exactly the loser, or should not have seemed such. After all, he was the politician getting his way. He was the self-righteous protector of the 'rights' of the fox, asserting his party's dominance over the legislature. But Michael still looked flea-bitten as he led the canter towards the hunt ban. He still looked miserable, mangy, weak.

Perhaps I should have invited him along to the hunt that Saturday morning. He might then have seen some of the damage his ban has done to the delicate balance of agreements and respects which create a law-abiding, consensual society.

The crowd at the hunt, both on foot and on horseback, was a broad social mix of taxpayers. The meet's host was a doctor, a general practitioner who devotes his working life to the reduction of human suffering. Doctors are paid by the state and are often held up as the greatest of our communal servants.

The doctor fell into conversation with the huntsman, a rough-palmed countryman with a Marches accent and a healthy contempt for urban legislators whose animal rights laws only worsen the lot of country animals. One of the many nonsenses of the hunting ban, for which the nowadays highly political RSPCA lobbied hard, is that it has increased the pain suffered by foxes. To die at the teeth of a hound (the kill comes with a single bite) is surely less grisly than to die after hours of blood loss from an imperfectly aimed rifle, as preferred by New Labour.

What values are these, precisely? Should ill-informed, emotive arguments really defeat common sense? Yet that is what Alun Michael achieved.

In the crowd at the meet I also recognised farm hands, students, a surveyor, the wife of an Arabian Gulf oil worker, a taxi driver and a part-time undertaker. Mothers placed toddlers on to the backs of Shetland ponies. Several in the crowd were churchgoers. There was even one church warden. All these people had come out in support of an activity which our elected legislators had decided to ban. What does that say about their legitimacy? What does it say about our respect for them and for our fellow voters? The Prayer Book, in its listing of the Ten Commandments, has us recite the words 'incline our hearts to keep this law'. Oops.

'We've got some antis,' I was told by an elderly gent with a walking stick – a gent, it should be added, who does much work for local charity and was once a significant employer in the area. He sounded worried, as well he might. A couple of months earlier his wife, a keen hunt follower in her mid-sixties, was on the M5 heading south to Devon when one wheel on her horsebox fell off and nearly caused a fatal crash. She discovered that the nuts had been loosened by 'antis' at an earlier meet.

These 'antis' were, for many years, the unlawful disrupters of a lawful activity. Now, officially, the equation has been reversed. The 'antis' are the ones on the side of the law as it is written. The hunt followers are the ones engaged in the illegal activity. However, it is hard to imagine any hunt enthusiast stooping to the depths of loosening an opponent's wheel nuts. We once lived in a world where the criminal and the disreputable went hand in hand. These days, thanks to Alun Michael, things are more complicated. The people engaged in the legal activity are the ones who behave badly. An hour later I was driving the girls home and we saw the antis clambering in and out of hedges, dressed in military fatigues, Army binoculars round their necks. All male, they made a threatening sight and they were spying on, as it happens, our land. The girls were frightened by these shadowy figures. They have heard about bad men who prowl and snoop. Such are the allies of New Labour. Such are the people who donated a million pounds to Blair's party to get him to do their bidding and make hunting illegal.

The police were in attendance that hunt morning. I approached them to say hello. They were friendly and mingled happily with the hunt supporters. No law was at that moment being broken by the hunt (it is not, yet, against the law to eat sausage rolls and drink mulled wine on horseback) but I don't think many of us were fooled. There was a distinct possibility that a fox might well, later that day, find itself being pursued by hounds in contravention of Alun Michael's daft law. And yet, as I say, the police were there in a benevolent capacity. Far be it for me to suggest that they were in any way condoning illegal hunting, but their approach was certainly not of the 'zero tolerance' nature so frequently claimed by Home Office ministers.

I was glad that my daughters were more interested in the Quality Street chocolates being passed round the crowd by a much-decorated female war hero than they were in asking me why the police were supporting an illegal activity, why a crowd of grown-ups whom they had been reared to respect were assembled in celebration of an outlawed sport, and why any Parliament should have so tarnished its own standing by giving house room to such a ridiculous and impractical ban. When they are old enough to ask such questions I shall have to refer them to the Rt Hon. Member for Nonsense Central, Mr Alun Michael.

33 Rupert Murdoch

No freelance journalist writes idly about Rupert Murdoch. It is not that the old fox himself is too twitchy about his reputation. His commercial success is enough to inoculate any man against self-doubt. Criticism of Murdoch, however, tends to worry his flunkeys and grunts. All those suited Osrics and Igors of the corporate world – the managing editors, the executive twisters – fly into vengeful fury on behalf of their distant princeling.

Murdoch ownership of many media outlets has been efficient if sometimes a little discombobulating. *The Sun*, the *News of the World*, BSkyB, even *The Sunday Times*: all have benefited from an injection of Aussie populism. *The Sun* does more for adult literacy than any government initiative and its jaunty humour is a corrective to the piety of today's ruling clique. Has *The Sun* made our politics more vulgar? Well, yes, probably. But another word for 'vulgar' is 'unstuffy'.

One issue of *The Sunday Times*, meanwhile, contains almost as much clobber as the entire Internet and Sky News gives BBC News 24 a run for its money, or rather our money, whatever you think of rolling news.

Politics without Murdoch would be less frenetic, more smug. In the United States a diet of the unreadable *New York Times* and the anaemic *Daily News* used to be unbearable. Along came the Murdoch-owned *New York Post* to knock Manhattan's prudish liberals off their plinths. The man from Oz partly serves the same purpose here, although he has more competition on the right of the market. It is possible to argue that one institution Murdoch dislikes, the monarchy, has been strengthened by his assaults. Murdoch has made the Royal Family more realistic about their role and the expectations of their subjects.

The exception to all this bracing Murdochery, however, has been *The Times*. When Murdoch bought the paper it was close to moribund. Its editorial reflexes were as slow as the heartbeat of a hibernating tortoise. It seldom thundered, preferring soft murmurs in a decaying dusk. Yet *The Times* remained distinctive. It represented a journalistic extreme (albeit one of fogeyish scholarship) and was still, or tried to be, the 'paper of record'. It maintained an accuracy which restrained the rest of Fleet Street. *The Times* gave British life a particular flavour – a stately, English, stiff-collared honesty. That has been mislaid under Murdoch.

The old *Times* ran long, informative but unashamedly un-newsy profiles of Whitehall mandarins. It quietly noted disasters and coughed polite disappointment when others wailed. It was the journalistic embodiment of understatement, holding a shrewd but modest idea of its own worth. To have a letter published in *The Times* was to lick a teaspoon of ambrosia, its correspondence page being the pre-eminent forum for lay debate. Today's *Times* letters page is no longer that acme. It carries a lot of letters from public relations people and the 'jokey' contributions are rather overdone. The paper's change to a tabloid format crushed the elegance of the letters page. It lost its status. A Britain without an authoritative, tightly edited *Times* letters page is somehow a less civilised place to live.

To compound the diminution of the old order the Court and Social page and the obituaries – once a noticeboard for society's doers – were banished to a distant realm towards the back of the book. The leader column also changed. The old *Times* editorials may not have been immediate but they were expert, freighted with classical and literary allusion, seasoned by a calm worldliness which only said 'something must be done' in the most urgent cases.

There was less of a place on the old *Times* for blatant political greasers. *Times* writers were expected to reach a conclusion using their own skulls and then stick to it, unhysterical but well reasoned. The sub-editors were admirable pedants. The news pages were shielded by rigorous filters, pap and spin soon being winnowed out. It is hard to imagine, in the old *Times*, the political writer being a slovenly, foul-mouthed sucker at the teat of Downing Street – yet that is exactly what happened in the high Blair era. One can think of a couple of glistening warthogs, wait-and-see merchants of the worst degree, who have used columns in *The Times* to advance not only their own prospects but also those of their political patrons – and devil take the reader.

Today's *Times*, you see, is indisputably a Murdoch paper. It trims to the guvnor's aesthetic, even if he does not directly order it to do so. Second guessing the boss: that was the name of the game sometimes in recent years – although the new editor seems to have retrieved matters somewhat. This *Times* has been in hock to marketing, poppy in its selection of photographs and vacuous in its appraisal of celebrity. It has plugged other parts of the Murdoch business web and obeyed its corporation's creeds. It has quivered rather than stood proud, head shrouded by clouds. Murdoch's *Times* has been pretty much identical to the other main daily newspapers and yet it has continued to live the lie. *Times* readers have been invited to believe that they are buying a straight-down-the-line organ of record, a descendant of the organ run by Dawson and Haley and Rees-Mogg, the 'top people's paper'. Murdoch's *Times* does not have an ideological heart. It used to be Thatcherite and then backed Blair. It has kowtowed to the decision-makers of the day in Whitehall (and Peking), shedding honest belief in favour of the opportune and the convenient. During Thatcherism it downplayed the perils of the Prime Minister's radicalism. Under Blair it shrugged off the corruption, the rupturing of decency, the moral idleness of the ruling elite.

It may now have a few hundred thousand more readers. It may be a more competitive newspaper in terms of features and giveaways and distribution. But those gains have been at the expense of something more intrinsic, something which moulded our national life and made it richer and more mature. *The Times*, alas, has lost its soul. Let's hope the new editor can rediscover it.

34 John Prescott

When Al Capone was brought to justice it was not for murdering rival mobsters. He was not busted for bootlegging or racketeering or riding the running boards of a polished Chrysler, Tommy-gun blazing as he chewed the wettened end of a sulphurous cheroot. Gangster Al was undone, instead, by a comparatively minor shortcoming with his tax returns. He was let down by an avoidable detail.

The same can be said of John Prescott. Come to think of it, there are certain similarities between Prescott and 'Scarface': a tendency to portliness, a love of grandiose motor cars, even a proclaimed 'common touch' and certainly a ready eyebrow for the girls. Capone started working life as a barman. Prescott was once a ship's steward, curling his lip as the ocean liners rose and fell on the briny swell.

Prescott was the most gormless and ineloquent person yet to hold the non-office of Deputy Prime Minister. This so-called statesman spoke English like a bibulous chimp. In his Labour Party conference speeches he cranked up class hatred in an era when most adult Britons were trying to place such social insecurity behind them. The Labour activists cheered his grammatically sub-normal, spleen-laced gruntings, but they were cheering a ghost of their political identity. They encouraged Prescott because they felt bad they had moved to the Centre. The poor were suffering! Tax the rich! So taxes were discreetly raised and the people who got hit were the lower middle classes who had recently managed to better themselves and rise off society's canvas. Prescott's demand for social justice pushed their noses back down on the floor.

Prescott traduced journalists for having the temerity to write the truth. He swore at women, even while calling them 'luv' like the old-fashioned sexist he was. He debased himself and his rank by thumping a member of the public in the 2001 general election campaign, by bedding his secretary, by flicking V-signs on the steps of 10 Downing Street and by licking the plate of privilege until it was almost spotless.

In the final days of his pomp he rode the system, running up vast expenses on the state tab with a foreign trip of little discernible public value. He would not have been out of place in the Chinese political elite he so liked to visit. The 'Comrade' bit would certainly have come easily to his flubbering tongue.

In all these matters Prescott, a revolting specimen with the manners of a flatulent caveman, demeaned our public life. He was an ape, an ass, a snake, a sour, sneering, snarling jackal. Nor was he any good at his role as supposed keeper of the Old Labour flame. Tony Blair laughed at his knuckle-headed deputy. New Labour patronised its working-class No. 2.

Prescott was placed in charge of transport policy and promised to reduce the number of cars on the road. More buses! More tax money! The number of cars went up almost as fast as taxes on the petrol which took long-suffering Mondeo man to work. Prescott tried to impose his desire for a north-east of England regional assembly on an underwhelmed electorate. More tax money! More money for working people to yield from their shrivelling pay packets. But in that case Prescott received a sharp blow to the hooter when the electorate said, 'No thank you'.

The one area in which Prescott claimed success was the relationship between Blair and Gordon Brown. Dinners, with Prescott as arbitrator, were used to keep the two men on speaking terms. But might it not have been better for Britain if Brown had been smoked out? Was the extravagant Brown's uncontested inheritance of the Labour leadership – a fruit of Prescott's peacekeeping efforts – really a good move for our politics? Or was it a sign of the rottenness of the regime?

And then we reach the small detail – the Capone fault, if you like. At 3.31 p.m. on 7 March 2000, Prescott rose in the House of Commons to make a statement on planning. He declared that he was 'putting in plan policies that will radically alter the way in which we build new homes in this country'. He had a funny way of pronouncing 'homes'. It came out as 'hormes'.

One of these policies was a change in the demands made of developers and planners. In future, Prescott said, 60 per cent of new 'hormes' would have to be built on 'brownfield sites'. At first glance this seemed an admirable suggestion. The layman, listening, would have presumed that this Prescottian policy would lead to new housing on old industrial sites, derelict warehouse land, rotting wharves, defunct quarries, etc. Alas, what no one in the Commons that day seems to have realised, 'brownfield' sites included the back gardens of workers' 'hormes'. And with Prescott imposing high building targets on local authorities, particularly in the south-east of England, that meant one thing: the destruction of shrubberies and lawns, the desecration of the one piece of greenery many salary slaves might hope to glimpse in their battery-chicken lives.

Since that speech in the Commons thousands of back gardens have been developed. Suburban homes which once had small dollops of greensward are now being pushed up against in-fill housing. Songbirds have been robbed of their habitats. Children have lost their kickabout spaces. Rainwater has been denied open ground – with the result that storm run-offs are now thought to be a major contributor to increased flooding. Once again Prescott had thought he was doing the right thing, helping to create new homes for the toiling masses. Once again his solution created a few millionaires and worsened the lives of millions of others.

John Prescott, the would-be working-class hero who was photographed leaning on a croquet mallet on the lawn at privileged Dorneywood, turns out to have been the unwitting idiot who, rather than tell Tony Blair he should halt the immigration which was creating such housing pressures, instead legislated for the destruction of Metroland's lawn. Bang went the quality of much lower-middle-class life. A comprehensive disaster at the hands of a comprehensive fool.

35 Nicholas Ridley

here was a certain magnificence in the arrogance, the verve, the sheer bloody-mindedness of Nicholas Ridley. He said what he thought, even if it was likely to upset the electorate – something we have largely lost in today's politicians. He smoked like an East German Trabant. He happily attacked his own party's backbenchers. And as a young minister he took the risk of resigning from the Government (that of Edward Heath), saying that he did not agree with the Prime Minister's big-state industrial policy and would therefore not accept his offer of the Arts Ministry, such as it was. This principled resignation would later stand Ridley in good stead with Margaret Thatcher, but it cannot have seemed a great career idea at the time. It took courage.

So, there were traits to welcome in Nicholas Ridley. He would no doubt have made an agreeable travelling companion, combative with petty officials and enough of a Renaissance man (he was a good watercolourist) to paint any vista worth recording. He would have been an inspiring, if mercurial, army officer, one whose moves the enemies would have found hard to predict. Had he turned to headmastering he would surely have produced interesting pupils prepared to challenge orthodoxies and create a truly 'vibrant' community instead of the homogenous pap of a culture which has been forced on us by conformity, the national curriculum, approved methods and the various other mealy-minded dictates of 'liberal' Leftism.

Sadly, Ridley went into politics. Even more disastrously, he became Secretary of State for the Environment at the bitter, wild, deluded height of the Thatcher era. The radical Ridley, his mind aswirl with free-market theories and a disdain for inaction, was placed in charge of the one thing which, above all else, needs caution and quietude: the English countryside. It has never recovered, nor probably ever will.

Ridley came from an old landowning family but he was the second son. This meant he did not inherit the Ridley mansion and thousands of acres in Cumbria. Maybe that rankled. Maybe that made him determined to bugger up the shires – particularly the South, which he never much liked – for everyone else. He certainly seemed to set about that goal with gusto once he acquired the necessary powers.

Ridley, whose aristocratic drawl disguised a Cromwellian contempt for the old order, became Environment Secretary in 1986. He arrived at the Department after three destructive years at Transport, where he had approved the expansion of Stansted Airport, the wails of local residents against this rape of the fields of Essex being flicked aside as casually as some of the ash which habitually fell on to Ridley's lapels from the sixty Silk Cut he smoked each day. 'I put enjoyment in front of health,' he would rasp, when chided about his smoking. 'I don't think people should be harassed in these matters.' Hear hear, many of us part-time libertarians will be tempted to say. But Ridley's live-today-and-damn-the-consequences philosophy extended to his view of the English countryside. There was no sense of stewardship in his politics, of looking after an inheritance for future generations. The second son in him, you see. He was in it for himself, not for the family estates, which in the case of an Environment Secretary means the national landscape and environmental balance. Ridley did spawn three children but there was seldom much evidence that he worried about the world they and any offspring would inhabit.

At Transport he also allowed the Okehampton by-pass to be carved through a national park and pushed ahead with bus deregulation, a policy which promised to improve bus services and save the government money. Has it achieved those aims? Hardly. Ridley's unswerving attachment to free-market economics did little except create a few private bus-company millionaires and push former passengers into the cars which now clog up our roads and by-passes. Car ownership was held as a great thing by the free-market Tories. Public transport was too communal – socialist – for their tastes. It was something no successful person over the age of thirty touched if possible.

At Environment Ridley's trust in private enterprise and disdain for public checking mechanisms led to a surge in urban sprawl. Local authorities learned not to engage in legal battles with land-hungry developers, for in case after case which went to Whitehall for adjudication the Secretary of State, an instinctive opponent of councils, awarded heavy costs in favour of the private companies. Sidmouth, Devon, still bears the scars of Ridley's rule. In 1989 a building company finally, after years of opposition from the council, secured planning permission on meadows just outside Sidmouth. A beautiful approach to the town, acclaimed for its tree-lined splendour, was wrecked by an eyesore development of bungalows. Fear of a swingeing adjudication from Ridley was given as a reason for the development being allowed to proceed.

Restraints on building over farm land were eased by Ridley, leading to vast edge-of-town supermarkets and the ruination of town centres with their small, farmer-friendly food suppliers. Old rhythms of life were being crushed by the zealot at Environment. Some Conservative backbenchers tried to tell Ridley he was wrong. They told him that his building plans were unpopular. Ridley sneeringly dismissed their concerns and called them 'NIMBYs' (Not In My Back Yard). But is it not a proper duty of MPs and their constituents to protect their own patches? NIMBY-ism is arguably nothing less than environmental activism by another name. Soon afterwards Ridley himself, with despicable hypocrisy, objected to a planning application on land at the bottom of his garden in Gloucestershire. Those refined principles, flourished so publicly when he left Heath's Government, suddenly appeared less prominent.

Everything was being done in such a rush. Although he liked to profess himself the opponent of Marxism and big planning, Ridley was allowing the face of provincial England and its market towns to be changed rapidly, to the extent that housing estates were knocked up with insufficient provision of shops or services. The closes and crescents of these new, *Neighbours*-style developments had as much sense of community as the vast accommodation blocks of the Soviet Union which Ridley liked to attack. State supremacy was merely replaced by the supremacy of profiteering builders.

As Environment Secretary Ridley also allowed Peter Palumbo, a property developer better known for his social connections, to pull down one of the City of London's most distinctive and popular fixtures, the cheese-slice Mappin and Webb building. Ridley was an admirer of modern architecture, its sharp new lines sating his appetite for destruction and change. Really, he was not a Conservative at all. He was a wrecker. A leveller. A force for upheaval and upset, and as such the unwitting ally of self-enriching business executives whose high-profit box dwellings would have horrified Ridley's grandfather, the architect Edwin Lutyens.

Nicholas Ridley, in some ways such an engaging figure, embodied the worst of Thatcherism. He mistook neglect of duty for hands-off government and we will live with his mistakes until the weeds of Doomsday lift their tendrils and bring man's ugly brickwork cascading back down to earth.

36 Geoffrey Rippon

Like many amateur yachtsmen Ted Heath resented the professional seafarers of the trawler fleets. Nasty, smelly, working-class brutes, their vessels threw out a hefty wash which must have sent *Morning Cloud*'s cologne bottles flying. How it must have stung when they laughed at the rope-sandalled bachelor Heath and his boaty boys.

Perhaps that is why Heath leaned on Geoffrey Rippon and ensured that Britain's fishing fleet was thrown overboard when we joined the EEC. For lean on him he most certainly seems to have done. Rippon, being a stooge, did as told.

Geoffrey Rippon was a stolid figure little given to displays of mirth or self-doubt. In certain lights he had something of Ted Heath to him, though without the jocular shoulders and the artistic temperament. He was thickset. He was a suburban form-filler. He was an appeaser of other people's agendas. Rippon, the sometime Mayor of Surbiton, was a pettifogger on whom the demands of duty weighed heavily – almost as heavily as did the desire to remain in Prime Minister Heath's good books and do whatever the Europhile cause demanded.

Rippon was made Britain's chief negotiator on entry to the

European project soon after the general election of 1970. He had originally been made Minister for Technology and was put out to have been given such a runt of a job by Heath. Having earlier had something of a reputation as a rightwinger (when it looked a sensible thing to be, careerwise) Rippon had sucked up hard to his piano-tinkling leader during the Opposition years. Surely he had played the game enough to deserve something better than mere Technology. The sudden death of Iain Macleod created vacancies in the new Government, however, and Rippon, with his Coke-bottle specs and broad bottom, his dull speechifying, his smooth managerialism, inherited the European negotiator job from Anthony Barber, who had been promoted to Chancellor.

Soon Rippon was immersed in the protracted cave-in to the national interests of 'The Six' – the European countries who had already formed the EEC. The self-regarding manner of European political grandees suited him. He started to take the view that politics was not the business of representing and enacting the people's desires. It was the business of by-passing populist sentiment for the benefit of a bureaucratic cabal.

Fishing was a problem. Fishing was a British strength. Yet the Europeans were insisting that we join a Common Fisheries Policy that they had just whistled up. Fishing presented a possible block to progress to a more united Europe because it was an industry with a loud voice (all those throat lozenges, you see) and because it was hard to see how any concession on fishing could be presented as beneficial to our national interest. Rippon and his controller Heath therefore resorted to lies. Their attitude seems to have been one of 'don't let the little people understand how much we are surrendering'.

Rippon told the 1971 Conservative Party conference that, 'one thing is certain – we should not sign a Treaty of Accession which would commit us to the present fisheries policy'. Well said that man! He told the House of Commons soon afterwards that 'there is a clear understanding that either we must have an agreement on a new regulation – or the Community will have to accept that we must maintain the status quo'. Well said again!

Come the hour of New Year's Day, 1973, however, our fishing rights were handed over like mackerel snagged in a net. All Rippon had managed to retrieve (after heavy pressure from Heath to concede to French demands) was a temporary arrangement which expired in 1982. It was a different story in Norway, where a similar deal was proposed and refused, not only by the Norwegian fisheries minister, who quit, but by the electorate, who were able to see more clearly what had happened and declined to join the EEC. Had Rippon been braver and placed his own short-term job prospects on the line, Britain's once prosperous fishing fleet might have been saved. An industry that once employed almost 50,000 people would not have dwindled to near nothing.

Despite his cowardice Rippon did not last long in power. Heath's Government was hurled from office. Rippon bit the dust when his patron vanished as Tory leader. He had overdone his sycophancy. Heath's successor, Margaret Thatcher, regarded Rippon with the scorn he deserved. He went off to become a lawyer, a City fat cat and a director of Robert Maxwell's publishing company. Oil finds its level.

Europe was not the only evidence of Geoffrey Rippon's preparedness to destroy and appease – or of his arrogant assumption that the ways of the past could only be improved by modern ideas. As Minister of Public Buildings in 1963 he casually announced that he had 'decided to abolish' the Foreign Office's Italianate edifice in Whitehall. Designed by George Gilbert Scott in the mid-nineteenth century, it was a remarkable symbol of high imperialism, both solid and ornate. Rippon was unable, or disinclined, to appreciate its beauty. Maybe the associations with Empire displeased him. Maybe he was simply doing the bidding of cunning radicals in his Department who had convinced him that this was a way to 'make your mark, Minister'. Anyway, he announced that it would be razed to make way for a new, forward-looking building. Only the loud protests of Sir John Betjeman and the Victorian Society prevented Rippon from having his way. What a pity they could not have saved our fishing industry, too.

37 Charles Saatchi

Iraq-born Charles Saatchi has done more to foul up Britain than Saddam Hussein managed before he went swinging from his gibbet. Saatchi is the former advertising executive – lowest of lifeforms – who is credited with an infamous 1979 poster suggesting Margaret Thatcher would solve unemployment. The image of the dole queue and the slogan 'Labour isn't working' may have been clever. It may have won votes. But it was little better than a lie. Mrs Thatcher's policies put millions out of work and the repercussions of that high unemployment are still evident twenty-nine years on.

Having thus proved his credentials for honesty, as a man we could trust, this Saatchi turned himself into an art dealer. Not that he quite called himself that. He preferred to describe himself as a 'collector', that word conveying something more refined, selective, even philanthropic. He also started to project himself as a recluse, if that is not an oxymoron. Air of mystery, you see? Good for the brand.

In this guise Saatchi set new standards for depravity in public taste, which distorted the London art market, and made himself not only richer but more famous (all the more so when he married the ripe widow Nigella Lawson, whose first husband was the peerless John Diamond). Saatchi was the hermit with the hunch, the loner eccentric who had the nose for art. The sheep of the media followed him, followed by the bleating masses of the art market. If the rumour went out that 'Charles Saatchi is buying Carruthers' or 'Saatchi thinks Smythe is the next hot thing' then money cascaded into those artists, often allowing Saatchi to sell his initial modest investments for gains of many multiples. This was all a great success for Charles Saatchi. However, for British art – for British aesthetics, British values – it was a rather less fortunate episode.

Saatchi is the man who 'invented' Britart, the phase of modern art in this country which drove traditional artistic skills to the margins and ignored the concept of beauty. If a society loses its idea of what is beautiful it tends to lose its grip on good behaviour. What are manners if they are not a quest for a form of beauty? Why should any child behave itself if the adults are refusing to conform to ideals and standards? The adolescent, seeing how artists can claim that an unmade bed is a valid example of artistic expression, need never again listen to the imploring commands of his parents.

Art is not just about the personal whims of 'collectors'. It is, when shown in public, a community matter and Saatchi, who asserted that he was interested in art so that he could 'show it off', is every bit as much of a public figure as an elected politician. It is no coincidence that the spread of Saatchi's sensationalistic art tastes coincided with a period of horrible delinquency in our lunar-pockmarked streets. A good example of art reflecting society? If you insist. But has art no responsibility? Do art patrons not have a duty, with all their money and their education, to try to improve the world around them and try to lift their fellow citizens' noses out of the vomit-filled gutters?

Saatchi's taste for the decade that started in 1992 was for filth, violence, controversy at any cost. Phallic obsession often came into it, as did death and disease (David Falconer's 'Vermin Death Stack', a ten-foot pile of dead mice, was perfect Saatchi fare). If the pursuit of such deranged, unpleasant, godless tastes meant upsetting the respectable parents of a teenage girl who had died from drugs, so be it. If it meant glorying in the death of Princess Diana, cool. If it meant crushing the morale of artists by dropping them as fast as he had taken them up, tough. Saatchi was in it for Saatchi, not for society, nor even for some idea of art. Saatchi couldn't give a toss. Iraqi Saatchi is like that.

He made the careers of such deadbeats as Stella Vine, the 'artist' who drew an immature, unskilled painting of young Rachel Whitear, a Herefordshire schoolgirl who died from drugs. Rachel's parents, as if they had not already been subjected to enough pain, found the stunt 'abhorrent'. Saatchi's protégé Vine was unapologetic. She said she was 'really sad about the timing' and didn't think how Whitear's parents would react. The painting came 'from love and from passion and I'm not going to stop making art'. More's the pity.

Then there was the case of a Saatchi work which was ascribed to a thirteen-year-old girl, Naomi V. Jelish, whose family had allegedly disappeared after her father drowned. The media scented a tragic tale. It turned out that Naomi never existed and that the art, if art was the word for it, had been created by a Royal College of Art graduate called James Shovlin. 'Being a Scrabble bore I saw that James Shovlin was an anagram for Miss Jelish,' said the languid Saatchi. A Saatchi 'spokesman' added: 'It is not a deceit. It is an extraordinary, complex piece of art.'

Saatchi does not seem to care about the corrosion he has caused to our values. When a country sees the likes of Damien Hirst make millions from pickling sharks and from the sort of 'homage' (with his collection-box girl) that cruder minds might call straight plagiarism, its inhabitants form the view that honest endeavour is a mug's game. Does Saatchi never stop to consider what it does to the nurse or the soldier on a basic wage to see such fecklessness as Tracey Emin's 'Everyone I Have Ever Slept With' hailed as a masterpiece? Where is his civic sense of purpose? But Saatchi is rich enough not to have to rely on society. Like the businessman in Anouilh's 1947 play *Ring Around the Moon* he thinks he can simply buy any human he likes.

Some defenders say that 'at least he got us talking about art'. But what is the point of talking about art if the art is not up to it? The only good thing about Saatchi is that he is such a 'gorger of the briefly new' (as he puts it) that he quickly falls out with his collaborators and this, in turn, has weakened the solidarity of the Britart crowd. Many of them now dislike Saatchi. Welcome to the gang, guys! Saatchi also seems to have fallen out with the other giant squid of modern art, Sir Nicholas Serota. What a happy pairing they make, two vast egos competing for the title of 'most important munchkin in modern art'. Along with Serota, Charles Saatchi has been responsible for a demoralising infection of our national aesthetic. Decadence has spread. True artists, who have conquered age-old skills of painting and sculpture, have practically starved in the Saatchi-twisted market. Impressionable commissars have drifted in his direction. It has all been a wheeze, a passing fancy, a lucrative con which, for all the talk of 'democracy' and 'populism', has enriched a handful of elitist dealers.

Oh, Nigella. How *could* you?

38 Sir Jimmy Savile

Like the lavatory cleaner Harpic, Jimmy Savile is a 'household name'. Rather a peculiar one at that. Savile did many things in his career, from ballroom manager to hospital porter in a loony bin, but he is best remembered – with a shudder – as a determinedly ageless presenter of children's television shows.

There are other examples – Tony Blackburn, Sir Paul McCartney, Keith Chegwin, Chris Evans – of egomaniac idiots whose refusal to submit to age infects our society with immaturity. But Savile, this heavily bejewelled Peter Pan who seemed to have great chunks of polished metal riveted to every appendage of his withered body, was the worst. He epitomised a breed of shallow show-offs whose refusal to grow up cheapened the currency of authentic, heady youth.

We can ask if such a creature would be allowed anywhere near today's primetime children's shows. Tune into a children's TV channel nowadays and it is rare to find anyone quite so old, so white, or with such wriggly eyebrows. And in an earlier age James Wilson Vincent Savile would have been consigned to a touring circus or end-of-pier show. It was his good fortune to be born (October 1926) just in time for the early days of

post-war mass television when controllers were looking for 'characters' – a euphemism for shameless bores.

Savile wore his hair long, of a colour not quite white, nor quite yellow. If certain of its strands did appear to have a custardy hue it may have been because 'Jimmy' was a keen smoker and his fringe had been stained by the nicotine.

His wardrobe was designed to be so disgusting as to get him noticed. Savile was the villain who introduced the shell suit to the British public. For that alone he is worth pillorying. He was also, with Elton John, a proponent of novelty spectacles which, being something of a wit, he would lift up and down while yodelling in his Yorkshire accent. When Eric Morecambe did this it was funny. When Jimmy Savile did it you wanted to lift the spectacles off his nose and place them under your heel.

Son of a bookmaker, Savile started admirably enough as a Bevin Boy coal miner but found that life underground ill suited his hunger for publicity. The 1950s found him managing the Mecca Locarno ballroom in Leeds, sidling up to customers and enquiring if they were 'all right, chuck'. Oh, you are naughty, Mr Savile! The way you make them bulge, so.

No, no, Dolores, not his underpants. His eyes. The way he makes his eyes bulge.

Savile was one of the last TV presenters to get away with licking an enormous cigar, his long tongue darting out to linger appreciatively on the wet end of the stogie. To do this on children's shows was quite a feat. Supporters of the tobacco industry will commend him for a valiant stand against the anti-smoking lobby, or at least they might be tempted to do so. But then they might remember that the same Jimmy Savile, far from being a hero of the anti-health and safety resistance, is the man who fronted the 'Clunk Click' campaign of TV commercials which bossily instructed the British people to wear seatbelts in cars. Savile was prepared to tell people how to save their lives, when, paradoxically, many of those passengers saved from car crashes would go on to suffer long, painful deaths from tobacco-induced lung cancer.

Savile also fronted adverts for the nationalised British Rail. Passenger numbers hardly boomed. Maybe it was the horror of thinking Jimmy Savile might be in the train compartment.

He was briefly a racing cyclist and a wrestler, two activities noted for their sweatiness. He did a spell as a hospital porter at Broadmoor, where his presence at the tea urn may well have sent patients even further off their trolleys. 'Nurse, nurse, quick, this man keeps talking in a terrible yodelly Yorkshire accent. Syringe me, please. I can't bear any more!'

In 1960 fame beckoned when he landed a job fronting a TV show, *Young at Heart*. Savile was by this time well into his thirties, when most men of that age were rooted and well embarked on middle adulthood. My father, roughly the same age as Savile, was assiduously trying to rear his family and adhere to the standards of the pre-permissive England. Yet there was Savile, behaving like a halfwit, pulling down the temple for his own greater glory.

He dyed his hair a different colour for each week's episode, even though the programme was broadcast in black and white. What a card! By the time he presented the first edition of *Top of the Pops* in 1964 he was very nearly in his fifth decade. And yet he addressed the audience of youngsters almost as a kindred soul. He slung his arms around their teenage waists. He pulled silly faces. He behaved more foolishly than anyone else in camera shot, even though he was easily the oldest geezer on the set. His presence blurred the true zest of the young and made it something creepier. There was an air of 'happiness is compulsory' about him that was both irritating and, in its way, political. His act withdrew the sense of public permission for thirty-year-olds to be square and sensible.

Savile is one of the few people to have appeared twice as a subject on *This Is Your Life*. It is said that the production team responsible for the second programme were unaware he had been on the show before – he has been around that long. He is a member of Mensa, teetotal, likes to jog, lives in a 'bachelor penthouse flat', and still has his late mother's clothes dry-cleaned once a year (he called her 'The Duchess'). He may well have 'issues' with death.

We should note that he has raised a great deal of money for charity and, in the process, helped improve hundreds of lives. He was duly knighted. That very nearly earns him the clemency of the court – an official pardon, no less. But then we remember his crazed insistence on youthfulness, his impermeable resistance to the dignity of old age, and the projection of himself as a talisman of youth, even while driving round in a Rolls-Royce with HIS1 number plate. The man is a maniac. Guilty as charged!

39 John Scarlett

John Scarlett is head of MI6 but he shouldn't be. In a country with a surer sense of political shame he would by now have retired to the bursarship of a minor public school or maybe the reins of a firm providing mercenaries to dodgy dictatorships in western Africa.

Scarlett is the intelligence expert who allowed Downing Street publicity pedlars – the headline and bullet-point men – to stick their oars into the drafting of the 'September dossier' about Saddam Hussein. Britain later became enmeshed in America's war with Iraq. It may be too strong to say that Scarlett alone pushed us into that unpopular war which has caused thousands of deaths at a cost of billions of pounds. It is certainly fair to say, however, that his conduct left open questions about his impartiality and the way Tony Blair's Government used the state's secret services.

What is the value of an intelligence expert whose advice is not at all times chillingly dispassionate? What is the point of a security adviser who descends into group-think? Wars are best declared when every reason for *not* fighting them has been exaggerated, rather than vice versa. Battle should never be joined on the advice of a man of whom it may later be suspected that he was saying what the Prime Minister's clique wanted him to say – at a time when a promotion was in the offing.

Scarlett is just that man. He is the former British spy chief in Moscow who later became a 'mate' of Alastair Campbell and was dragged into the Hutton Inquiry row. At the inquiry he insisted, in front of the world's media, that he had taken the editorial decisions on the dossier. He had 'ownership' of the dossier, we were assured.

Reports of the evidence suggested this was not entirely the case, and that there had been an element of 'co-ownership', to put it mildly, with Blair and his snivelling thug Campbell. Yet Scarlett was believed by the old-world Judge Hutton and the Blairites amazingly carried the day. Their regime was saved. A short while later Scarlett was promoted to head of MI6.

For years our intelligence chiefs were anonymous figures generally known only as 'C' or 'M' or some other letter from the alphabet. It worked well that way. Personal glory and individual grandstanding were removed from the equation. A sense of continuity was established. No widespread kudos could attach to the people who held these important and sensitive jobs.

The anonymity meant these positions could not be handed to certain people as a public reward. Gesture politics could not infect the appointment of the men or women who ran the security services, for gesture politics depended on publicity and publicity was something the British secret services rightly spurned.

John Scarlett's prospects took a tumble when, after postings to Nairobi and Paris, he was expelled from Moscow in 1994 in a diplomatic row. His cover was blown when, landing back in Britain, he was photographed wearing a hat and a grin. That image, seen today, is one of a debonair man, rueful yet still ambitious. He looked – and still looks – like a maverick. Should mavericks help governments decide whether or not to go to war?

Scarlett's career was dwindling when Tony Blair appointed him chairman of the Joint Intelligence Committee in 2001. This position is effectively the PM's personal link to the intelligence network. It is not known when Scarlett first met Blair but he now had easy access to Blair and his acolytes, and they to him. A relationship flowered. The MI6 training should have prevented Scarlett from becoming too attached to his professional acquaintances but when it came to the preparation of the September dossier he seems to have been exceptionally accommodating. He let Campbell contribute ideas to the dossier which helped to make the case for the invasion of Iraq. Scarlett's staff told him in an email that Downing Street 'have further questions and answers they would like expanded ... No. 10 wants the document to be as strong as possible.' Scarlett told the Hutton Inquiry that he 'found it quite useful to have presentational advice'. He admitted that a 17 September 2002 memo from Campbell amounted to 'requests for changes'. Campbell took issue with the use of 'may' in a sentence which said that 'the Iraqi military may be able to deploy chemical or biological weapons within forty-five minutes'. The next day

Scarlett told Campbell that 'the language . . . has been tightened'.
When the dossier was released to the press several newspapers
focused luridly on this forty-five-minute claim. Did they do so
independently or as a result of prompting from Campbell and
Co.?

No. 10 wanted the dossier to be stronger on the nuclear
threat. One of Campbell's sidekicks, Tom Kelly, said in an email
that 'the weakness, obviously, is our inability to say that
[Saddam] could pull the nuclear trigger any time soon'. Were
these people not interested in objective advice? Why were they
pushing for 'strength'? Should Scarlett not have upbraided them?

At another point in the drafting process he sent out an email
to colleagues which said: 'I appreciate everyone, us included,
has been around some of these buoys before, but No. 10, through
the chairman, want the document to be as strong as possible
within the bounds of the available intelligence. This is therefore
a last[!] call for any items of intelligence that the agencies think
can and should be included.'

The September dossier was primarily a work of media
manipulation. The claim that Saddam could deploy his weapons
in forty-five minutes or less came from a sole Iraqi informant.
The BBC's Andrew Gilligan also relied on one source for his
allegations. *He* was duly mauled for doing so. Scarlett, who
even let Campbell chair one meeting on the dossier, was made
head of MI6.

That mild-mannered man Iain Duncan Smith, leader of the
Conservatives for much of the run-up to the Iraq War, has
called Scarlett a 'lying shit'. I would change the adjective. I

would change it to 'cowardly' or 'conniving'. It still seems amazing that he and Blair got away with their casual embellishment of the case for war. Why were they so close? It is a question that deserves investigation – perhaps by the head of MI5, or by the next head of MI6.

40 Howard Schultz

Once upon a time, not so long ago, it was routinely possible to buy a cup of coffee for the price of a popular newspaper. It was possible to buy that coffee in a container which did not contain nearly a pint of liquid so scaldingly hot that it was undrinkable for at least ten minutes after you had bought it. Once upon a time.

In those happy days the coffee container (beaker, to use the modern preferred term – though not preferred by me) did not have the name of the café printed all over its exterior. Nor did it have a white plastic lid complete with a tiny hole through which you were invited to sip the viciously blistering coffee on your trudge back to the office.

It was possible, in those halcyon days, to drink coffee without risk of cardiac palpitations owing to the wild caffeine jolt from the muddy liquid on which you have lavished what feels like a mortgage. Coffee used to be strong only if you ordered an 'espresso' or a 'café solo' or, to use another specialist term, 'a small Greek jobbie'. Ah, once upon a time. The time before Starbucks.

Starbucks coffee shops and their many imitators have run rampant across our island, teaching Frasier Crane-style

pronunciation to British youngsters and drying out our kidneys until they resemble old shoe leathers. It is hard to find the main street of a town in Britain which is not equipped with at least one Starbucks or Café Nero or Coffee Republic or Costa Coffee where impressionable youths ask with casual boastfulness for 'double mocha macchiatos' or 'lattes' (the long 'a' being quite wrong).

A plague on these Americanised, swanked-up coffee shops, their inflated prices, their corporate didacticism, their fake aura of homely intellectualism and their unBritish flavours. They are worse than McDonald's or Kentucky Fried Chicken because they pretend to be alternative and interesting. It's also the posey-ness, the smugness, the air of assumed oneupmanship with which Starbucks customers sashay down the pavement, beaker held forth so that the rest of the world can see that horrid green logo.

Before Starbucks arrived – the first reached our shores only in 1998, though it feels an age – our country was well stocked with 'greasy spoon' cafes. These had white tile walls, chrome ashtrays and pleasingly rounded, red, plastic containers which squirted tomato sauce on to your egg and chips (and sometimes, in fact quite frequently, on to your tie). Oddly enough the teaspoons in 'greasy spoons' were seldom greasy. Their fried bread was, though. Hmmmn. Heaven.

Starbucks does not deal in fried bread. Half the people there look as though they have never in their lives encountered fried bread. What a deathless prospect.

In a 'greasy spoon' the entertainment would be provided by a blaring transistor tuned to BBC Radio 2. An Embassy Number

One might be found slowly burning in the proprietor's fingers as she leaned against the counter, her low, swollen bust slowly melting the Bar Six biscuits arranged next to the push-down till. In a Starbucks, as in other modish coffee houses, any entertainment is crafted and approved by Head Office, just like the menus, just like the prices and the items of community news on a noticeboard designed to global headquarters' stipulated standards. So much for the community bit. The skinny boys and girls behind the counter may have perfect teeth and Californian lilts to their accents but individualism has been expunged. Instead there is just this ghastly argot of West Coast America.

Starbucks has a corporate mission statement. Of course it does. These sort of creeps always do. 'Establish Starbucks as the premier purveyor of the finest coffee in the world while maintaining our uncompromising principles as we grow,' it states. Note the ersatz quality to the language, the attempt to be seen as 'purveyors' (think eighteenth-century St James's) rather than mere floggers of hot drinks (twenty-first-century globalisation). Behind this mission statement there are 'guiding principles to help us measure the appropriateness of our decisions'. Oh, for God's sake. They're only a chain of coffee shops, yet they try to make themselves sound like a political party.

Principle two, since you ask, is to 'embrace diversity as an essential component of the way we do business'. Diversity? From a business with such rigid branding? As many a dizzy Starbucks customer might say: 'Puh-lease!'

All of which brings us, at last, to our subject: Howard Schultz. Starbucks was started in 1971 by a writer, Gerald Bowker, and two teachers, Jerry Baldwin and Zev Siegel. They opened a shop in Seattle which sold coffee beans and grinders. They pooh-poohed the idea of brewing coffee on the premises and selling it as a drink. They felt that coffee was better brewed at home.

The business did OK but it was never going to conquer the world. That was fine. The owners were happy. It was not until 1987, when Starbucks was bought by the remorselessly ambitious Schultz, that the drinks side of things took off. Businessman Schultz set about global domination. In 1995 the company conceived a 'Synergistic Rollout Program' under which one new store was opened somewhere every day. They did not open a Starbucks abroad until 1996 (Tokyo). Now look at them. Not even the grey squirrel spread and bred this fast.

Once it was Nazi Panzers which rolled through the avenues and *banlieues* of Western Europe. Now it is Starbucks. The trend may well pass. The British public may well, in time, tire of paying so much money for a mere cup of slop. Starbucks is not much more than a corporate brand placed in the hot frother. Brands are notoriously fickle things. They can go out of fashion as quickly as they came into fashion. So we must not despair.

But for the meantime Schultz, with his mission statement and guiding principles and his steamy broths of branded 'beverages', is the king of the caramel macchiatos and there seems to be nothing to stop the ruddy man. Unless he drinks one too many of his filthy brews and has a fatal seizure from all the palpitations.

41 Julia Smith

Three or more times a week BBC Television serves up a melodramatic – hyperdramatic – picture of our society which manages to be both out of date and insistently 'topical'. *EastEnders* bastes Britain in the juices of misery, violence and nostalgia, all in the name of public broadcasting. Public wrist-slitting, more like.

This depressing soap was devised in 1983 by the late Julia Smith, a drama producer whose earlier work included episodes of *Z Cars*, *Doctor Who* and *Angels*. With *EastEnders* she and a script-writer, Tony Holland, set out to portray London as it was at the time. What an appalling place London of the middle Thatcher years must have been.

Twenty-five years on we are still being subjected to the basic recipe of East London disgruntlement and selfishness, long after the caravan moved on, long after the white working class shown in these plots was overwhelmed by other cultural identities. The characters on *EastEnders* still talk Cockney, even though younger Londoners long ago took up a rap-music, street jungle patois which is heavily black American in tone. You seldom hear that sort of dude talk on *EastEnders*. Barbara Windsor and Diddy Puff don't exactly mix, I guess.

EastEnders doesn't seem much plugged into the Britain of mosque madmen or Barratt Home-aspiring young professionals. Where are the shrewd ethnic minorities with their community centres and their strident political identities? Have the makers of this programme ever actually *been* to the East End of London? Ah yes but, we are told, this is a drama about modern Britain. OK. So where are the dithering eccentrics of the ambling middle classes or the great swathe of young, concerned parents, or the volunteering *Guardian* readers, or the campaigning political activists, or the sober joggers, or the early-to-bed, churchgoing brigade? They exist in most communities but not in damp, demoralised Albert Square. Where, most of all, are the denizens of British office life, gaoled in their company towers for much of the day, to emerge in the evenings in suits, with briefcases and heads dulled by company routines? The only working people you usually see in *EastEnders* are market stall holders and barmaids.

This would all be very well for a drama were it not for the way that BBC executives try to use *EastEnders* as a vehicle for their own consciences and politically aware campaigns. Julia Smith cannot be held directly accountable for this, not least because she died in 1997, but she created a programme which has become the beast of burden for numerous 'issues' which the corporation's high-ups feel 'must be aired'. *EastEnders* has become a terrible vehicle for public 'awareness'. Homophobia, drug addiction, Aids, cot death, domestic violence, euthanasia, agoraphobia, bipolar disorder, breast cancer, alcohol abuse, teenage pregnancy, divorce stress, rape – all have been flung into the pot to keep the viewers perky. Perhaps it is no wonder the characters are so down in the dumps. They keep on being subjected to unspeakable worries by a BBC drama department which is itself frantic to keep people watching. Perhaps one day they will get round to a storyline which shows the desperate lengths people will go to when they are subjected to pressure about TV ratings. Now that really could be instructive.

Drip, drip, drip, this goes into the nation's psyche. Smith and her colleagues always said that they were merely reflecting the 'gritty' country we have become, but that was disingenuous. Such a regular application of primetime depression eventually eats into the national morale and turns us into the sort of population shown in fictional Walford. So much violence eventually becomes the norm. So much bleating and so much heavy sighing eventually become national mannerisms. You only have to hear the drumbeats of that brilliantly gloomy theme tune to be cocooned in a world of blunted ambitions and urban resentment. Give me *One Man and His Dog*, any night.

Few characters in *EastEnders* laugh. Humour is one of the most British of characteristics, yet it bats well down the *EastEnders* order of favourite gestures, long after scowling and jaw clenching and general whiney crossness. They really are the most frightful bunch of whingers. Is it not time they were put out of their misery?

Gobby Janet Street-Porter is the squawking embodiment of 'yoof'. She may herself now be sixty yet she still presumes to speak for the nation's twentysomethings and is forever moaning about how these precious flowers are being undervalued by the 'Establishment' to which she so clearly belongs.

Where this tall, vociferous bully has gone striding, shrieking at the gale about youth and its imperatives, a multitude of lesser media executives has followed. These over-the-shoulder glancers have swallowed Street-Porter's fractured, discordant view of the world. They have presumed (because they spend the rest of their time in meetings and know little of the world into which they broadcast) that the young and the untested are 'the way forward'. Janet shouted her creed of 'yoof', placing a ridiculous premium on novelty and frivolity. 'Yoof let it be,' came the feeble-minded response from media land. And with that, countless moronic shavers and dollybirds were catapulted on to our screens and into our consciousness, demeaning themselves, souring public taste and disfiguring national life at the expense of professionals who knew a great deal better.

This noisy, noxious Street-Porter, sharp-elbowed love-child of Sir Max Hastings and Sister Wendy Beckett, espouses a world of temporary façades. She craves a country where the young and the new and the shocking and the abrasive are automatically promoted over reliability, experience, wisdom, high seriousness. She is – naturally – a supporter of go-ahead architecture and its demolition balls. She throws her invective at tradition and moderation. She vents fury like a ghetto blaster whose volume knob is stuck on maximum.

The only ancient who deserves to be heard and listened to with respect, in her world, is Mrs Street-Porter herself. She is now in her seventh decade yet still seeks out the company of thirtysomething models and pop stars and their toothpastey boyfriends, grinning and gripping, seizing them whenever a camera is nearby. She seems to be terrified of old age and is that sad specimen, if we can have such a thing without upsetting butchers: mutton dressed as ham.

She has long ceased to act her age, much though she might sometimes wish she could. Perhaps she has a deep, dirty secret: a desire to retire to bed early at night with a mug of Horlicks and a slice of Dundee cake. Who, after all, can honestly claim never to have hankered for such pleasures? But Janet has to go on partying, showing us how energetic and 'sexy' she is.

Her marital record has been of a piece with this butterfly nature: four times married, four times divorced. It's only surprising that her husbands stayed with her long enough to make their vows. Were they not 'so yesterday' by the time they reached the register office? Those four unions were childless.

Had she been a mother she might have had a less irresponsible, sweeping, impractical picture of 'yoof'. Like many an ideologue she lacks experience of that on which she preaches.

This bellowing beanpole, with her Stonehenge teeth and loudhailer larynx, has been a Pied Piper for life's floaters. She has encouraged the vapid and entertained the undiscriminating who do not pause long enough to consider what she is doing for communal values. She has misdirected the impressionable and pulled down the temple around her large ears. She is as bad a totem to silliness as we have had in the past fifty years and it is greatly to be regretted that when Soviet scientists closed the doors on Sputnik 2 on 3 November 1957, they did not have room for 'JSP' in addition to Laika, the first dog in space. But maybe Laika's last hours were horrible enough without being subjected to that voice.

Mrs Street-Porter is, at her core, little more than a newspaper feature writer. Takes one to know one, believe me. She turns an acid phrase for a living. Outrage is just a position to strike, a lucrative pose. All that outspokenness is just a brand, minted for a living. That, you see, is the great thing about modern architecture and fashion. There is always some new atrocity to discuss. They keep Janet in gravy. She does not necessarily have to believe a word of it but it will pay her bills and ensure that she continues to be invited to trashy minor showbusiness parties where she can be photographed in gaudy outfits, baring her walrus gnashers to the lens and 'avin a really good larff'.

In public she disdains tradition. Yet the neophiles of the post-war generation have acquired their own customs and received attitudes, most of which our heroine adheres to with gluey predictability. To hear her on, say, the politics of George W. Bush or hunting or Prince Charles is to encounter an entirely orthodox new Establishment position. She may claim to scorn tradition and not give a 'faaaaaaack', what people think of her. The sorry truth, however, is that she is far less brave than she thinks. Many of her opinions are off-the-peg metropolitan views. She simply makes them sound different because she speaks in such a jagged, revolting voice.

This ageing non-revolutionary helped to mould a London media elite who are now hooked on youth. They consider youth a greater commodity than long-acquired expertise. They produce programmes, such as *Big Brother*, which seldom contain a face older than thirty, even though Britain's old-age pensioners are the biggest age group, and growing. The young, uninteresting and frequently unoriginal, are placed on a pedestal which should be reserved for the aged. While China remains a gerontocracy we have become a culture of cretinous juvenilia, mostly thanks to a sixty-plus freelance hack who fancies she can hold back the Grim Reaper by going to parties with Kate Moss.

43 Margaret Thatcher

Many of Margaret Thatcher's political decisions improved our country. She revived the acumen of our business tycoons. She prevented the Falkland Islands falling into the hands of a murderous junta and reminded us it was worth being British. She took a painful but wise decision to weaken the Unionists' grip on Northern Ireland. She allowed taxpayers to keep more of their earnings and enabled council tenants to buy their homes.

It is also claimed that the Thatcher Government 'saw off the unions'. This is not true. The trade unions have since crept back to prominence. Fighting trade unions is like trying to kill stinging nettles. You think you have won but once your back is turned they return with smaller, sharper stings, subtler but no less unpleasant.

It was in the pursuit of the trade unions – specifically, the National Union of Mineworkers – that Mrs Thatcher did lasting damage to our country. Her opponent in that bitter dispute, Arthur Scargill, was a mercurial Yorkshireman who deserved a bloody nose. He duly got one but not before he had convinced a large part of the North of the United Kingdom that he was

the victim of a southern Tory Government plot. Snivelly, ranty Arthur, son of a communist and owner of an inexcusable comb-over hairdo, may have cost his trusting members their pit jobs. He may have lost the strike itself. But before he faded from public life he persuaded many Northerners to sympathise with at least part of his message.

Impressionable millions listened to his theory about the Southerners doing in the North and, thanks to Mrs Thatcher's unyielding harshness, they found it plausible. The North–South electoral divide slammed into place like a prison door. Before the miners' strike began in 1984 it was not unusual to find Conservative MPs north of the Wash. Yorkshire towns such as Bradford, Leeds, Calderdale, Kirklees were solid Tory. Even Sheffield was blue in parts. There were Tories in Scotland, Tories on Merseyside and around Newcastle. It was possible in the 1970s and early 1980s to be both Conservative and traditional Northern. But not since Mrs Thatcher nailed Scargill to the cross. With the miners' strike the Tories lost great swathes of the North for a generation and since 1997 the country has paid heavily.

There are numerous excuses for Mrs T's rigorous pursuit of the NUM. The miners had wrecked the Heath Government and she did not want that to happen again. They were industrial has-beens led by a politically suicidal maniac who could not be allowed to succeed. All true. Yet there was something hungry in the way she persecuted the war. Her radicalism may have turned her into a political character but it had an ugly, vengeful side. Think how much more skilful her friend Ronald Reagan or the media-savvy Tony Blair would have been handling such a strike.

Mrs Thatcher was herself a Lincolnshire yellow belly, so hardly 'Southern', yet she played into a Northern Labour trap and it has constrained her party ever since. The Conservatives may not regain power until they concede that the miners' dispute was handled too sternly and mercilessly by their beloved former leader. It is time they acknowledged the hurt which, right or wrong, the North feels. Yet so swivel-eyed are the lady's ageing boosters, angry men with the lingering regret of deserted *matelots*, that any move to disown her handling of the strike would result in an angry convulsion. Such is her political bequest.

The coal miners themselves should not have been a target for Mrs Thatcher's ire. They were a remarkable body of men who did unspeakably tough jobs with great stoicism and humour. They supported their families and had a strong sense of community and patriotism. They had the sort of social values which Mrs Thatcher herself could and should have recognised. She failed to project any such understanding. She under-estimated and undercherished her opponents. She was insufficiently politic in her pursuit of victory and the subsequent closure of nearly all of Britain's coal mines makes it hard to deny that the Government intended, all along, to wreck the country's coal industry.

Labour has since poured public money into the North. Had Mrs Thatcher spent only a fraction more at the time, and been more generous in her attitude to the vanquished pit men, it could have saved us billions in the public subsidies which have since been ladled on the region. These have helped to turn it into 'Labour's heartlands'. State spending now accounts for nearly 65 per cent of all income in the north-east of England, and about 55 per cent in Scotland and the north-west of England. This blatant attempt to buy votes would not have been attempted but for Mrs Thatcher's obdurate behaviour over the miners' strike. There are northern Members of Parliament who can still earn a round of easy applause by attacking the Thatcher Government – yet who secretly must thank the lady for their seats.

To see how emotive a subject the miners' strike remains you have only to visit the musical *Billy Elliot* in London's West End: artful propaganda feeding on perceived victimhood. I'm sorry to say that Mrs Thatcher created that sense of pique and unless Cameron's Tories get down and grovel it will last for many more score years.

44 Alan Titchmarsh

To attack Alan Titchmarsh may seem an act of unwarranted violence, like aiming a water cannon at an occupied pram or dumping a gallon of the most toxic weedkiller on a lone dandelion. TV's Alan Titchmarsh? The man is just so darned 'nice'. So harmless. Isn't he?

When he restricted himself to gardening programmes Alan Titchmarsh was certainly no great threat to the nation and its sanity. But like mint in an English ''erbaceous border' (as our Alan would call it) or plantain on a 'manicured lawn' (Alan does love a cliché) he has run rampant through the television schedules, herpes on the lip of a promiscuous teenage girl. That jaunty little topknot of hair, that chirpy smile, those practised Yorkshire vowels. They're everywhere. Alan on *The Nature of Britain*. Alan on *The Great British Village*. Alan's *Melodies for You* on Radio 2. Alan's ITV chat show. He's more prevalent than the municipal begonia.

After an apparently blameless childhood on the edge of Ilkley Moor and an apprenticeship at the local nursery Titchmarsh first imposed his puppyish optimism on an unsuspecting public on BBC1's *Nationwide*. 'I suddenly tasted

blood,' he has said of those early appearances. 'It was – "Wow! I like this, I want to do more?"' Tasting blood? What is he? A horticulturist or a vampire? A Venus fly trap, maybe.

He was invited to share some radio airtime with Gloria Hunniford, which a late friend of mine, most uncharitably, once described as being like 'diving into a swimming pool alongside a great white shark'. It obviously wasn't anything like that as Titchmarsh progressed to that high temple of taste, the daytime television show *Pebble Mill at One*. As with goosegrass in compost, Titchmarsh took root. He thrived.

Gardeners' World, once a serious, unshowy programme, was given the Titchmarsh treatment. Its former air of restraint, of knowledge worn lightly on the smock, was discarded in favour of something more pally, more forced. The word 'my' was replaced by the word 'me'. 'Here we are in me garden,' Alan would say, squinting at the camera as though it was all an enormous joke.

The learned, calm tone set by Percy Thrower, Peter Seabrook, Geoff Hamilton, was yanked up and replaced by more gaudy blooms. Gardening was no longer permitted to be a quiet, soft-spoken, relaxing affair. Gardening had to be a riot. A hoot. It was a vehicle for Alan Titchmarsh and his comic aspirations. Titch was itching to make his mark.

His horticultural knowledge may be undeniable but he spreads it as thin as Marmite. There have been more than forty gardening books. Forty! It is a production rate almost to equal that of Anthony Trollope. Can he really have written them all himself or were 'researchers' involved? Has Alan Titchmarsh become a brand? Surely not, for that would clearly be at odds with his image as an honest, plain-talking chump. But his personal website, complete with its tempting offers on novelty watering cans and his assiduous mention of charities, is in keeping with a Maoist cult of the self.

Soon the gardening TV man tired of mere plants and greenhouses. Alan's agents told him that he was 'a personality'. They thought he should capitalise on his 'charm' – a charm which has left his wax figure at Madame Tussaud's 'the most fondled' of all the exhibits there. BBC controllers desperate for an easy fix to the ratings hit on 'a great idea' – a makeover programme called *Ground Force*. Maybe it could do for the corporation's viewing figures what it claimed to do for people's gardens. Under Titchmarsh's stewardship of *Ground Force* the ghastly craze for decking took hold. Any parts of suburban greenery which had not already fallen victim to Alan's love for pampas grasses and 'water features' were now sacrificed to the sound of Tommy Walsh's rivet gun and the saw of cheap wood. Ugh, *Ground Force*. Merely mention the programme's name and that irritating theme tune comes to mind, along with Cockney Tommy's grumbling, the swinging dugs of mad Glastonbury girl Charlie Dimmock, and sequences of speeded-up film as the producers desperately tried to inject an element of false tension.

What 'characters' the presenters were, the embodiment of spray-on change and of instant improvement – and as such a betrayal of the most fundamental necessities for any gardener, which are patience and the nourishment of the soul from slow, seasonal change. Alan Titchmarsh offered the gardening equivalent of fast food.

Does he care about the rhythms of the year, of the pace of Nature? Titchmarsh the multi-media star certainly has no time for such idle concepts. Professing himself a Christian, he popped up – 'popped up' is a very Alan sort of thing – on Sunday night's *Songs of Praise*. Taking the view that not even the youth of Britain should be spared his brilliance, his nasal, wheedly voice was to be heard on *Gordon the Garden Gnome* on CBeebies. Back on *Ground Force*, meanwhile, poor old Nelson Mandela pottered home one day to find that Titchmarsh and Co. had wrecked his garden. Sometimes it must be very trying to be Africa's best-known statesman. All these foreign celebrities trying to muscle in on your fame, and even changing your garden when you were perfectly happy with the way it looked. How he must miss that cell on Robben Island sometimes.

Titchmarsh is middle-road mediocrity made flesh. He is twee on two legs. He is comfy, bland and he has left television gardening uninformative and babyish.

On, on, on surged Titchmarsh, leaving behind broken dreams, imposing his twiddly idea of order. Soon he was to be found presenting everything from *Antiques Roadshow* to the *Paul O'Grady Show*. Need a man to make suggestive jokes – in an unthreatening sort of way, of course – about giant pumpkins on *The Great British Village Show*? Alan's yer man. He even found time to write fiction. There have been several novels, one of which won him the bad sex prize. Alan is also 'doing his bit for the environment' by joining the 'Saving Planet Earth' project. But after so much Alan Titchmarsh, will it want to be saved? Or will it plead for euthanasia?

45 Topsy and Tim

Jesuits were said to take the attitude, 'Give me the boy and I will give you the man.' They knew that ideas and attitudes, if planted with sufficient care in a young mind, would likely flourish and multiply. The Left has discovered the same truth. It seeds its creeds into the juvenile mind, not least through the medium of children's storybooks.

Few authors do this more relentlessly than Jean and Gareth Adamson, co-creators of the mystifyingly successful tales of Topsy and Tim.

Twins Topsy and Tim are sister and brother. They are aged five and have remained that age since they first blighted our culture in 1960. They live in a town and lead lives of blameless, centre-Left orthodoxy. They are possibly the most unexciting little children it will ever be your misfortune to imagine and yet their experiences – adventures is too strong a word – have been thrust down the throats of parents and toddlers for the past forty-seven years. The prose is execrably dull.

Topsy and Tim do not have markedly separate identities. This being the New Era, girls and boys must be considered the same. Sometimes it is Topsy who cries, sometimes wimpy Tim.

Sometimes Topsy kicks a football, sometimes Tim admires a flower. Oh look, a pansy.

These two little creatures are moulded for a world of unisex barbers and gender-neutral officialdom. In the stories of Topsy and Tim there is none of that Victorian stereotyping about girls liking pink and boys playing with worms. Good heavens, no. This is also true of Topsy and Tim's Mummy and Daddy. They share the household chores. Their bland characters are interchangeable. Mummy never succumbs to a bad mood. Daddy is never distant, or batey, or hungover. He never has a snort of hard drink in the evenings. Not much of an introduction to modern Britain, is he? How one hankers to write a photographic negative of Topsy and Tim, stories which show our debased country as it truly is – and worse.

In the world of Topsy and Tim grown-ups are like something out of a Liberal Democrat party political broadcast, devoid of hormones, never too fagged out to listen, always interested in the snivellings and witterings of their goody-goody progeny. These grown-ups are attentive to community needs and to the development of responsible attitudes among children. Most of all they are alive to the terrible dangers of the world. Health and safety and correct behaviour are the major threads in most Topsy and Tim stories. Car seatbelts are always fastened. Fireguards are always secured. Bottles of naughty poison are always locked in approved cupboards. Pity. Just a little glug, glug of it would get rid of these two prattleboxes once and for all.

When Topsy and Tim spend their first day at primary school

Tim 'astonishes' his sister by eating all his greens. No flicking peas across the dining room for little Timmy. No stuffing cabbage into his sister's pockets. When a bully called James commits a foul in a playground game and makes Stevie Dunton cry, some children disgrace themselves by joining in the mockery of Stevie who is pretty plainly as wet as a snipe moor. Not Topsy and Tim, though. No. They sneak on James to Miss Terry. 'He's always doing nasty things to Stevie,' says Topsy. 'He's a bully,' adds Tim. Right little couple of supergrasses they are. What a pity Miss Terry did not tell them to mind their own business and let weedy Stevie discover the school of hard knocks. Yet the story cannot give up on James. To do that would offend leftwing sensibilities. James needs to be understood. He is obviously a victim, too. And so it comes to pass that we find 'poor old James' is being abused by his mother and his big brother. No doubt they will be persecuted by social services and sent away for re-education.

When Topsy and Tim go to the seaside they stop, en route, for a picnic. A safe grass verge is found and at the end of the picnic two entire pages are devoted to the business of picking up litter from the site. Mummy gives them an empty carrier bag for the litter. A plastic bag? Oh no! This episode was clearly written before correct thinking turned against supermarket carrier bags. We must trust that this episode will be rewritten and that in future Mummy hands the twins a reuseable hessian bag bearing an eco-awareness symbol.

Over the years the soppingly damp stories of Topsy and Tim have, inexplicably, sold more than 21 million copies. There have been 130 books so far, ranging from *Topsy and Tim Meet the Firefighters* (not firemen, please note), *Topsy and Tim Have Itchy Heads* and *Topsy and Tim Learn to Swim*. Drat. There goes our chance of puncturing their armbands.

Despite that saying of the Jesuits I am proud to report that my children found Topsy and Tim dead boring. We had been given some of the books by my leftwing sister. There were only two ways to use them. One was as a punishment. 'Right, you ill-disciplined urchins, you've been so ruddy disobedient I'm going to read you *Topsy and Tim Go to the Dentist*.' Blood-curdling screams would ensue.

The alternative was to read a Topsy and Tim story in a satirical manner, with breathy voices and widened eyes. Our favourite for this was the *Topsy and Tim Safety Book*, when the twins encounter a long succession of hazards. What bores they are, never taking a risk, never daring to do something naughty.

A Britain peopled by disciples of Topsy and Tim would not last long in the world of international terrorism. 'Topsy and Tim Go to Afghanistan to Confront the Taliban'? If we succumb to the worldview of Jean and Gareth Adamson we might as well give up now.

46 Harold Walker

Labour MP Harold Walker was one of those pitiable fixtures in politics, a 'character' who was not quite as clever – or as popular – as he supposed. He may have convinced himself that he helped the conditions of the working man but Walker can be held responsible for that irritating, meddlesome, self-sustaining public body, the Health and Safety Executive.

Typically with Harold Walker, it wasn't meant to pan out quite that way. He was, as they say, only trying to help.

The throat-clutchers of Elf N Safety owe their existence to the Health and Safety at Work etc. Act 1974. The Employment Minister who pushed that Act into existence was Harold Walker. Health and Safety at Work is an 'enabling Act', a broad creation allowing other legislation to sprout under its span. European health and safety directives can simply be pushed into British law like extra passengers on to a train.

With his gummy grin and Mancunian airs Harold Walker was a convivial man. He was a regular of Annie's Bar, one of the more rheumy-eyed Westminster oases which has since closed its doors, owing not least to the fact that many of its regulars died of cirrhosis of the liver. Walker held his drink better than many and rose to become a deputy Speaker of the House of Commons. Quite a harsh one, too. But for Betty Boothroyd he might even have succeeded Bernard Weatherill as Speaker.

Walker demands our attention thanks to his enthusiasm in the early 1970s for health and safety laws. Two factors played hard here and help to place his actions in context. The first was the terrible number of industrial workers who at that time were being killed in accidents at work. Some thousand men were being killed a year in industrial incidents and a further half a million workers were being injured. The second factor was the power of the National Union of Mineworkers. The NUM had more clout than elected governments, as it proved when the Heath Government was felled in 1974. Few industries were as dangerous as coal mining. So that was why health and safety was such a hot issue at the time.

The Health and Safety at Work etc. Bill came to the House of Commons for its Second Reading on 3 April 1974. The Tories had lost power only two months earlier. Politicians, perhaps understandably, tiptoed round any industry-related issue. The Conservatives, with William Whitelaw as their frontbench spokesman, decided to give their support to the Bill and its creation of both a Commission and Executive to supervise Health and Safety.

The record of the debate (in which a youthful Patrick Mayhew made his maiden speech) is instructive. Legislators were concerned almost exclusively with heavy-industrial work conditions. They talked about mines and foundries and building sites. Agriculture was not directly covered by the Bill. Michael

Foot, opening the debate as Secretary of State for Employment, said that the Bill was designed to address 'matters of life and death'. That would be the area in which the Health and Safety Commission and its subsidiary the HSE would operate, he said. 'It is not our intention to set up a body which becomes remote from questioning in this House,' said Mr Foot. Today's parliamentarians who find that the HSE is almost impossible to hold to account may wonder at the chasm between intention and reality.

The Labour Government had taken recommendations from a comparatively moderate, light-touch report written by Lord Robens at the behest of Barbara Castle. Mr Foot boasted that the Government had beefed up Robens's suggestions considerably. The person credited with this strengthening of the proposals? Harold Walker.

Mr Foot acclaimed Walker as the Government's 'expert' on health and safety. A one-time toolmaker and shop steward, Walker was himself very much a tool of the trade unions. Unions saw health and safety not only as an essential safeguard for their members but also as a political weapon against employers. A skilful shop steward could easily engineer a dispute out of health and safety worries.

When his own turn came to speak, Walker expressed 'personal satisfaction' that his long years of campaigning for a Health and Safety Act had come to fruit. He spent a large section of his speech sucking up to mineworkers, another in promising juicy staffing numbers of the HSE, and yet another in trying to fiddle things so that only established trade unions would have a right to sit on safety committees. Walker also called for companies to be forced to include health and safety reviews in their annual reports.

Closing, Walker boasted about the Bill's unexpectedly draconian proposals and called it 'the most significant advance in health and safety at work since the 1830s'. He may not have been wrong about its significance, but long before he died in 2003 he must surely have been surprised at how the focus of Elf N Safety had switched from heavy industry, which has so dwindled, to offices, schools, domestic appliances and applications.

The Act proved the high moment in Walker's ministerial career and it would be another eighteen years before he failed to land the Speakership. A peerage followed, more as compensation than in recognition of his intellect. He died Baron Walker of Doncaster, of Audenshaw in the County of Greater Manchester, a stalwart of Doncaster Catholic Club, Doncaster Trades Union and Labour Club, Westminster Recreational Club and numerous other social outfits where old industrial workers might gather over a morning half-pint of bitter, perhaps to ruminate about the over-legislation of European directives and safety edicts which had driven so many of their old companies out of business. The Health and Safety Executive had proved a significant creation, all right, but one that in the end killed off many of the industries it had set out to regulate.

Harold Walker, the grandfather of the HSE, often meant well. But that is not quite the same as saying that he achieved good things. Not the same thing at all.

47 'Webonymous'

There is a harmless tradition of pseudonyms in print. *Private Eye* has its literary gossip 'Bookworm', its architecture critic 'Piloti', farming expert 'Muckspreader' and some parliamentary buffoon who goes under the name of 'Gavel Basher'. Bernard Levin wrote for *The Spectator* as 'Taper', although his work was so good it was pretty obviously Levin. Colin Welch and Michael Wharton shared the by-line 'Peter Simple', the invented persona not only allowing them greater creative width but also meaning they could take days off without the knowledge of their newspaper managers.

More elevated were the *noms de plume* 'George Eliot' (Mary Ann Evans) and 'George Orwell' (Eric Blair). We can think of 'Q' (Sir Arthur Quiller-Couch), Bulldog Drummond's creator 'Sapper' (H.C. McNeile) and the great 'Saki' (H.H. Munro). Pseudonymity is, clearly, an acceptable and even noble condition. Sometimes it has permitted a writer to step outside unreasonable social constraints, particularly in the days when women were not 'meant' to publish their work. Sometimes it is used to allow a contracted scribe to work for other employers (this is the reason for most of the *Private Eye* by-lines). The newspaper diarist, by working under a pseudonym, can operate 'under cover', gaining access to confidences. A diary column which is called 'Mandrake' (*Daily* and *Sunday Telegraphs*) or a 'Black Dog' (*Mail on Sunday*) can be more outspoken and upset powerful figures without alienating the specialist reporters who penned the items and need to keep in their sources.

The arrival of Internet blogging has changed the game. On the countless 'have your say' and 'what do you think?' slots on the worldwide web, particularly in the fields of arts criticism and political debate, pseudonymity and (more often) anonymity are now more common than open identity. This is wrecking the tone of public discussion. It is lowering it to the grottiest levels of invective and allows interested parties to present an unbalanced view of public opinion.

There used to be an old joke, 'Who is the most prolific poet in the English language?' Answer: Anon. The same Anon. is now the most prolific poster of pro-Government comments on political activists' websites. Anon. is always fast to defend films or theatre productions which have been pooh-poohed by the named mainstream critics. Anon. tends to ascribe the worst motives to those professional critics, always doubting their independence of mind, often seeing conspiracies.

Anon. is a bully – but a coward. Unlike the bloggers themselves, who may operate under their own names or may use a consistent Nom de Blog (e.g. Guido Fawkes, Recess Monkey, Madame Arcati), Anon. can zip in and out of the action and pose as someone different every time. It would be different if each Anon. had his or her own number, like South

American Volkswagen Beetle taxis. Then we could at least, if we were so disposed, chart the regular themes and paranoias of that particular Anon. We could say, 'Ah, there goes Anon. 154829647 again, sounding off about the influence of right-wing Christians at the BBC' (unlikely, but you never know). We could work out where each Anon. was 'coming from', which in turn would add or subtract weight from the arguments being made. But we cannot. Anon. shelters behind the shield. Anon., though happy to attack, is not prepared to defend. Anon. is a bit of a creep.

Anon. may often be a professional rebutter, perhaps a lowly paid member of a public relations firm employed by a West End impresario who is desperate to flog tickets for a bad musical which has cost millions of pounds to bring to stage. Anon. may be a full-time lobbyist, perhaps in the pay of the tobacco manufacturers or the animal rights brigade or the enemies of Israel. Anon. is certainly not proud of himself or herself.

Those of us who write under our own names in the newspapers are accustomed to receiving occasional, unsigned hate mail. At least those correspondents have gone to the trouble of buying a stamp. At least, too, they have stepped out of their houses to walk to the post box. That form of abuse seems more healthy than miserable Anon. crouched over a keyboard in, who knows, some foetid basement flat in the East Midlands, firing off angry words in the way that an unfortunate sufferer of psoriosis will scratch and scratch and scratch until eventually the blood is dripping down a scaly-skinned leg.

That's Anon. for you – the rage of modern Britain festering behind closed doors, too timid to stand by the words in public, just content to hurl vitriol and hide from proper argument. It should not matter yet, like gangrene, this acid dissent spreads and eventually overwhelms. Should freedom of speech not be reserved for those with names?

48 Tim Westwood

We may no longer rule the waves, have much manu-
facturing industry or strictly deserve a seat on the United
Nations Security Council, but there is one thing we British can
still claim to do better than other nationalities: speak English.
The Irish run us close for conversational zest. The Americans
are the ones who have nourished English as the world's foremost
language. But our island is the home fortress of this glorious
tongue and – at our best – we speak it with greater confidence
and clarity and verve and precision than other people.

No one 'owns' English but its current dominance of world
commerce and culture gives us an advantage. To squander that
– to do anything that made us less distinctive and less certain
in our speech – would be an act of monumental stupidity.
Wouldn't it?

Step forward Tim Westwood of BBC Radio 1, de cuckoo in
de nest. Middle-aged Westwood is a public-sector disc jockey
('public-sector' means we pay his wages) who has so immersed
himself in the music of black rappers and American-style hip-
hoppers that he has started to talk like one – and is leading
thousands of young listeners down the same ill-guided alley.

The result of his own dialect's drift is, to say the least, unlovely. He sounds more like a cross between an East Anglian farm girl and one of Biggie Smalls's roadies. But the fact that he makes such an effort to slough off his own accent and assume the no-neck argot of transatlantic ghetto rappers is significant. That flawed sound dropping from Westwood's thin lips, silly though it may be, imperils our cultural self-confidence and national identity.

Westwood is the son of a deceased Church of England prelate, Bill Westwood, who was born in Gloucestershire and worked his way up through a northern English curacy to become Bishop of Peterborough. We know that 'Bishop Bill' did not speak hip-hop because he used to do the 'Thought for the Day' slot on Radio 4's *Today* Programme and he sounded perfectly normal. There was not the slightest echo of gangsta gun runner to his thoughtful homilies. Nor is there any reason to suspect that kindly Bishop Bill married some 'ho from da hood'. Tim Westwood's mother is, by all accounts, a blameless clergyman's widow.

Part of Tim's childhood was spent in a bishop's palace. As a boy he was surrounded by politely spoken souls whose Anglican vowels and consonants reflected the England of Betjeman and Mrs C.F. Alexander. He may have been dyslexic at school but that hardly accounts for the remarkable transformation from bishop's son to rap-beat evangelist. It is hard to imagine someone with less in common with the likes of Snoop Dogg and 50 Cent. Those 'artistes' themselves may be fine upstanding men but their genre as a whole is only too happy to tolerate violence and a moronic tribalism which laughs at sexism and skulking menace. It is all a long way from the close of Peterborough Cathedral.

What happened to cause this transformation? Where was the street harshness of Tim Westwood's rearing? Where was the anger, the gender resentment, the ethnic anxiety, the urban roughness? Can this really be an example of repression leading to extreme rejection? Is a boyhood of occasional coffee mornings, weekly matins and flower-arranging rotas – man, all dem daffodils jes blew mah mind – truly such an ordeal? Or is Tim Westwood an enormous fake? Is Bishop Bill's boy bogus?

Westwood is said to be the model for the satirical character Ali G, that prize 'wigga' ('white nigga') who speaks in the gibberish dialect of the jewel-encrusted Los Angeleno rap guy while in fact being a white, middle-class nincompoop. Watch Westwood strutting his stuff for a few minutes and you are left with the uncomfortable suspicion that Ali G was in fact a dilution of the real horror. The satire is not nearly as grim as the real thing.

When Westwood wakes up in the morning are his first words of the day rapper-ish? Or does he, in his most private moments, speak still like a vicar's boy? When he talks to his old mum does he call her 'bitch'? If so, let's hope she gives him a good slapping.

Arrayed in West Coast America clothes and the ultra-clean training shoes considered *de rigueur* by hip-hop stars, Westwood does all those baffling rap-man hand gestures while he talks. You know the type of thing. He flicks out his little pinkies and throws his elbows in a horizontal line. He bounces from heel to heel when conversing (or rather, when lecturing – conversation implies a two-way process involving the desire to listen). He approaches the camera with a crablike gait that looks part-menacing, part-constipated. His sleeves are too long for his limbs. He frowns a lot. You'd never think this berk was almost fifty years old.

He talks of 'bigging up' his various acquaintances, of 'crews', 'cats', 'dudes'. When indicating an affirmative he spits out the words, 'zackly, man'. He wears the waistband of his trousers low on the buttock. 'Jes smoothin' out mah laydees wiv sum R an Bee,' he'll say. Roughly translated, this means he hopes to impress his popsies by playing them some romantic airs. Less alluringly, Westwood has even been shot at in his car by some of the deeply unpleasant elements who inhabit his part of da music world's hood. What a dreadful example he sets our young.

Westwood was a marginal figure (a joke in many ways) on commercial radio before Radio 1 hired him in 1994. It was the era of John Major's culturally retrospective Tory Government and Matthew Bannister, a careerist who was running Radio 1 at that time, perhaps thought he could earn himself some credit by doing something daring. Westwood's appointment was blessed by Director-General John Birt, incorrigibly dull and notoriously short of humour. Birt was always creepily desperate to get in with 'the young' and seems to have fallen for the absurd Westwood act. Who knows, they probably did the high-five to one another. Birt probably loved being called 'man'.

And so our state-sponsored broadcaster, whose privileged position is meant to be accompanied by a sense of values and community well-being, has given prime airtime for the past fourteen years to a hybrid weirdo who encourages our youngsters not only to listen to the filthy music of the likes of Eminem and Puff Daddy but also to speak in this disfigured, urban-aggro way that is unintelligible to the broad mass of British society. Impressionable teenagers think that this is the clever way to talk. In fact it is the surest route possible to unemployment and trouble. Westwood 'gives them permission', to use the psychobabble term, to drop their national inheritance of properly spoken, coherent English. If they follow his example they will end up being understood by few and employed by nobody. They drone on about 'respect' but by adopting rambling spiels of nonsense they disrespect the rest of society, not least themselves.

This is broadcasting not as a national service but as a sad spectacle, a bid to be thought trendy, a 'me-me' plagiarism of a damaging culture from another land. BBC executives desperately want to show how 'up' they are with hip-hop, yet they entrust it to a fraud whose message, in short, is that we should dump our linguistic heritage. The inauthentic Westwood is an emblem of cultural defeatism, of broadcasting decadence. Switch him off. Man.

49 Helen Willetts

Officer cadets at Sandhurst used to be taught which strategic facilities to secure during an attempted *coup d'état* in the colonies. The territory's airport, power station, main hospital, harbour and radio command centre were among the sites considered vital for state control, to be guarded by armoured cars and soldiers with berets.

What about cultural coups of the sort we have had in Britain this past decade? The targets are slightly different, ranging from the Arts Council to the morning news shows, the ruling sports bodies to children's television, but the idea is roughly the same. And near the top of any list of vital cultural installations? The BBC weather forecasting unit.

It is naïve to believe that weather forecasters are there simply to predict the following day's climatic conditions in as quick and clear a way as possible. Forecasters have become some of the most familiar faces and voices in national life. As a result they form the norm. They have become celebrities and entertainers but most of all symbols of what society – or its string pullers in the metropolis – accepts as the ruling average. Culturally, this makes them powerful.

Weather men and women, in their language, clothes and mannerisms, can be more subversively influential than any national newspaper. Since the mid-1990s the BBC, our publicly funded broadcaster, has been wilfully political in the way it has run weather forecasts on TV and radio. Presenters have clearly been chosen to project a cultural orthodoxy which is anti-conservative, anti-intellectual and plain babyish. Forecasters who offended the new aesthetic were moved to off-peak bulletins or allowed to 'retire'. The magnificently retro Michael Fish, with his kipper ties, comb-over hairdo and *Rising Damp* accent, blew off in the direction of the English Channel. John Kettley, who made the unforgiveable error of wearing a heterosexual moustache, was vaporised as fast as a summer puddle. West Country Bill Giles and his wink are now as distant a memory as one of last summer's showers.

Meteorological isobars were also shown the door. Who wants nasty scientific symbols which might actually help explain how weather arrives at our island shores? Pah! Millions of pounds were spent instead on a computerised weather map for TV forecasts, a swooping, rotating, multi-coloured device which left many viewers baffled and feeling distinctly air sick. Their complaints were waved aside, dismissed as the wails of reactionaries unable to accept the modern world.

In the place of Fish, Kettley and Co. and the stick-on cloud symbols which served the late Bert Foord so well, the BBC has inserted a cadre of pushy modernisers, many of them northern-accented show-offs who speak to the viewers as though they were sub-teen morons. The queen bee of the lot is a geeky-smiled creature called Helen Willetts, so patronisingly soppy that she should have been either a primary school teacher or a dietician at a fat farm.

Willetts, who parades her Chester accent with care, frowns at the tragedy of it all if she has to suggest rain is on the horizon. Sunshine is greeted as a marvel. Come snow showers she practically says 'brrrrr' and shivers her shoulders before telling viewers that 'it could be cold today, so do wrap up'. Wrap up? Yes, why don't you, Helen?

Sometimes the producers get one of their 'great ideas' and send Helen or her colleagues out on the road, to present the weather from an outside location which is loosely linked to a news story. All this ever does is allow Helen to utter some platitude about the setting before giving precisely the forecast she would have delivered had she been in the studio. The viewer is at best distracted, at worst driven to a frothing rage by Helen's trite observations and pristine gum boots.

Willetts is not the only one. There's Newcastle-born Sarah Wilmshurst, gulpy and cloying, inclining her head in sorrow when she has to report a possible drop in the mercury. Come the dread day that she gets bumped off the weather by the next generation, our Sarah should be able to find herself a comfortable second career as a hospital visitor, oohing and aahing to elderly patients as they tell her about their boils and bumps. On the male side there's wide-eyed, camp-as-a-daisy Daniel Corbett, clapping his hands together with cruise ship entertainer relish at the prospect of an incoming front of high pressure. Corbett is actually married – to a woman, moreover

– but it would not be hard to imagine him revolving a pair of nipple tassles at Madame Jo-Jo's nightclub, Soho. If he doesn't drive you into the consoling embrace of a lunatic asylum there's Chris Fawkes, maddeningly upbeat, so chirpy you can almost smell the mouthwash off him even when he's on the radio. Northern vowels crack off his palate like rifle shots. A keep-fit enthusiast is little Chris, keen (so his personal web page tells us) on tandem freefall parachute jumps over the New Zealand alps. Scissors, nurse, quick. Let's have a saw at those parachute strings. Rob McElwee considers himself something of a wit and drops his voice so low at the end of his sentences that half of his forecasts are inaudible. And then there's Alex Deakin, another keep-fit freak who has the utterly infuriating habit of closing each broadcast with an over-matey, 'and that's yer weather'. Yer? Yeurrrrrrrrrrrrrrrrrrrrrgh!

The only thing that can be said for these homogenised, fake-happy weather forecasters with their New Labour airs and baby boomer credentials, perhaps, is that they are not Sian Lloyd, she of the lip gloss and sticky voice on ITV. Sian is now a big figure in the celebrity magazines such as *Hello!* When she broke off her engagement to Lembit Opik, a Liberal Democrat MP, the Welsh media treated it almost like a royal divorce. Lembit is MP for Montgomeryshire but you won't often see that fine county on the weather map nowadays. Sian always seems to stand in front of it, no doubt to block the sunshine from Lembit's life.

50 Harold Wilson

From the way he sucked on that pipe you might have thought Harold Wilson a great ponderer, forever cogitating, theorising, thinking of ways to improve the lot of his fellow man. But the pipe was a prop. In private Wilson puffed plutocratic cigars. Fat Cohibas and taut Torpedos, rolled on the warm, moist thighs of toothless Cuban hags, are not the playthings of a philanthropic philosopher. They bespeak a more selfish sense of purpose – a 'me me' spirit rather than the benevolent father of the nation, cradling the warm bowl of his pipe as he scanned distant peaks for communal fructification.

Wilson was disinclined to do much heavy policy thinking himself. He darkly suspected the civil service of being a Tory conspiracy. He therefore hired others to do his thinkin' for him. Worse, he had their wages drawn from public funds. Harold Wilson was in some ways a good Prime Minister. He kept us out of the Vietnam War, not least. He was in at least one respect, however, a very bad premier: he created state-paid Special Advisers.

The existence of such despicable creatures as Jo Moore, the woman who decided that 11 September 2001 was a 'good day to bury bad news', can be traced back to Wilson. So can the foul presence of that steaming pile of partisan malevolence Alastair Campbell, the nightclub bouncer at the door of Tony Blair's Downing Street.

The Special Adviser is an appointed stooge, an outsider brought into Whitehall by a minister or political party. He or she normally lasts only as long in that department as the minister. Special Advisers are, by their very nature, short-termists. They tend to take decisions which help a minister avoid blame or trouble, usually at the expense of another minister, sometimes merely because the extent of a problem has been temporarily concealed. Special Advisers are antipathetic to openness. Secrecy gives them power.

Special Advisers increased slowly in number and prominence. Wilson had a small knot of them at No. 10 (about five) and his senior colleagues had one each. Edward Heath did some minor fiddling with Special Advisers (if we can put it like this) and made them answerable more to the Cabinet than to individual ministers. Margaret Thatcher, with her keen suspicion of civil service obstinacy, created something of a praetorian guard of policy-thinkers at No. 10 but was never particularly keen on Special Advisers sprouting uncontrolled throughout Whitehall. She preferred her junior ministers to use their brains. She was never quite sure if Special Advisers were 'one of us', either. So little time. So many colleagues to monitor for signs of disloyalty. What an exhausting life she must have led.

It was only under hospitable, hopeless John Major, when Cabinet ministers started to rediscover some departmental freedom and found they could mould policy with greater hope of eventual success, that Special Advisers became more self-confident. Arrogant youths, many of them, they would strut into newspaper offices a pace or two to the side of their bosses, dispensing business cards and massaging their own reputations. One of them, you will recall, was called David Cameron. Special Advisers started to become more prominent socially. They became better known as sources of press stories. They overtook backbench MPs in the unspoken table of political importance.

And then, in 1997, came the Big Bang for Special Advisers. The numbers suddenly increased. In 1997 there were thirty-eight Special Advisers. By 2002, bang, there were eighty-one of them, no fewer than twenty-six of them employed at 10 Downing Street on behalf of the Prime Minister. There was a 'policy directorate' and a 'strategic communication' team, there was a 'special events' quintet, a 'research and information' duo, not to mention a 'chief adviser on strategy' and a 'director of government relations'. There may also, for all we know, have been a special Special Adviser whose job it was simply to dream up fancy titles and make sure no one was doing anyone else's work – a demarcation tsar, perhaps. The Chancellor of the Exchequer had his own stable of young thrusters, including a 'Council of Economic Advisers', some of whom looked as though they had barely started to shave. Across the departments Special Advisers were now mainly youngsters on the make, starting their political careers, one eye on their current position, the other on the possibility of finding a safe seat at the next general election.

The many millions spent on their salaries may be irksome – a symbol of the waste and the stroking of the political cadre – but it was wee buns compared to the billions blown on other inessential parts of the public sector, often on the say of, yes, Special Advisers. And even more damaging was the way these Special Advisers corrupted our political system. Since the later years of the nineteenth century the British civil service had been a professional body. That is to say, it offered recruits a career of serious service. Entrance to the profession was possible only after rigorous examination and interview procedures. Civil servants were schooled to regard the nation as their employer. They worked for the long-term good of the country, the community, not for the good of whichever politician happened to be in power at any one time. G.M. Trevelyan, historian, wrote that the merit-based entrance procedures to the civil service removed it 'from the field of political jobbery'. Favouritism, nepotism and nudge-nudge-wink-winkism were trumped by measurable ability. These values slowly percolated to other parts of society. It wasn't a bad way to run a country, you know.

Tony Blair changed that when, soon after sauntering up Downing Street for the first time as Prime Minister, to be greeted by a rent-a-mob of Labour Party supporters who were presented as ordinary voters, he gave two of his Special Advisers executive power over civil servants. Special Advisers had previously been unable to issue commands to civil servants. They were a discrete part of the system – held at one remove from the career officials of Whitehall. Now Jonathan Powell and Alastair Campbell had executive rights over the Permanent Secretaries. The Cabinet Secretary of the time, Sir Robin Butler, could have kicked up a fuss. He was near the end of his career at the time and arguably had little to lose (except the Mastership of an Oxbridge college, which indeed duly plopped into his lap). Yet Butler accepted the increased power of Powell and Campbell. The pass was sold.

Thus did political jobbery return to government. And all because pipe-sucking Harold Wilson couldn't be fagged to do some thinking for himself. Thanks, Harold. Thanks a bunch.

Bubblin' Under

There are plenty of other people who have done their level worst to bugger up Britain – people who, even as we speak, are burrowing away below our nation's ancient footings. The following are to be watched. Closely. With a fly swat to hand.

Roman Abramovich – Grotesquely rich Russian whose injection of cash at Chelsea FC and overpayment of laddish players has distorted the economics of English football, even while continuing to lift thousands of pounds out of fans' wallets.

Kate Barker – Busy, busy little bee of an economist who is Gordon Brown's favourite authority when he wants to propose concreting over the south of England and covering it in cheap housing. Expect her in the House of Lords soon.

Sir Lawrie Barratt – This house builder is the big daddy of urbanisers – yet with astonishing brassiness took the oak tree as his corporate symbol. What? Because he'd flattened so much green land to build his little boxes?

Victoria Beckham – Why must she keep thrusting her pelvis into Britain's face? You're a success, girl. You're rich. Even though you were never much cop as a singer. Why not just retire gracefully and enjoy life?

Osama Bin Laden – Himself the spoilt child of privilege, this peddler of death fries the minds of impressionable British Asian boys – yet does not even have the courage to come out and do so in public view. Why not agree to an interview with Jeremy Paxman, O cave-hopping Sheikh? Scared, are we?

Sir Ian Blair – Metropolitan police chief under whose command London's police seem to have become decidedly trigger-happy. Bang, bang, bang. Oops. Clumsy me. Another suspect bites the dust.

Sir Terence Conran – Canny salesman who developed a plausibly smouldering manner, knocked together a few cheap sticks of furniture, and somehow managed to become a 'design guru'. Ah, design, the new snobbery.

Simon Cowell – Is there a surer embodiment of the selfishness and shallowness of today's network television and its fixation with derivative competitions than this overpaid nonentity?

Martin Crimp and Katie Mitchell – Playwright and director duo whose dehumanised productions feature growly ambient noise and absurdist misery. Sentimentalism, romance and plot are held to be signs of weakness. Happily their influence is fading – but not fast enough.

Felix Dennis – Apologist for hippydom turned sauntering multi-millionaire, Dennis is so self-obsessed that he has had a forest in central England named after him. Also owns that journalistic vulture, *The Week*, a scissors-and-paste job read by people too thick or indolent to read the real thing.

Andrew Dismore – Labour MP and personal injury solicitor who has used his position on the House of Commons backbenches to frustrate minor legislative measures which might have restrained the power of . . . personal injury solicitors. A telling example of his profession.

Mohammed Fayed – The man who never became Princess Diana's father-in-law and has since devoted much of his energy to besmirching the reputation of the Royal Family. Horrifying symbol of vengefulness.

Mel Gibson – Thirsty Hollywood ego who, in addition to having gamey views about Jews, was responsible for the ludicrously over-romanticised *Braveheart* which helped fuel Scottish devolution and could yet rupture the United Kingdom.

Sir Donald Gosling – After groundworks by one Hermann Goering, Gosling bought bombsites and turned them into the hideous multi-storey NCP car parks which uglify many a British town and charge you through the radiator grille to use them.

General Sir Mike Jackson – This Captain Bluff, maestro of cigarettey waffle, was in charge of our Army immediately after the Iraq War. Could – should – have been a lot louder in expressing his disquiet about the Blair Government's strategic errors. Only let rip at officialdom once he had retired and the pension was safely in the kitbag.

Sir Terry Leahy – He runs powerful Tesco so why is this fellow so dour, so mirthless, so unremittingly lean? Let some sunshine into your life, man. While taking the country to the cleaner you might have the decency to radiate some joy.

Anthony McPartlin & Declan Donnelly ('Ant & Dec') – Zapper! Off button, quick!

Sir Paul McCartney – Pin-up pensioner for the generation

that never accepted its adult burden. Oh do stop dyeing your hair, you Charlie. Do buy a proper pair of shoes, and do spare us the Peace OK codswallop. How richly he deserved that nightmare Heather.

Gordon Ramsay – Bullying of employees is regarded elsewhere as a character flaw but Chef Ramsay is applauded for his cruelty and his drearily profane language. Where is the pleasure in food with this crass cook?

Esther Rantzen – Abuse of children is terrible but might we be excused violent thoughts when a pair of teeth comes on TV, adopts a simpering tone, crosses two old nanny-goat legs, and starts lecturing us for the umpteenth time about how she founded Childline. What happened to anonymity in good works?

Richard Rogers – Over-privileged, over-rated, architect Rogers fancies himself a philosopher *de nos jours* and tries to pull political wires to assist his second-rank projects. What's amazing is not that his buildings are ever made but that this lisping old snoot was ever taken seriously.

Bob Shennan – This former BBC executive turned Radio 5 Live into a near parody of call-in shows and gobby, macho girl spoutery, hard news being placed second to under-informed comment and football obsession. Now he's gone, can we have some public broadcasting standards back, please?

Now try your own . . .

1.
2.
3.
4.
5.
6.
7.
8.
9.
10.
11.
12.
13.
14.
15.
16.
17.
18.
19.
20.
21.
22.
23.
24.
25.

26.
27.
28.
29.
30.
31.
32.
33.
34.
35.
36.
37.
38.
39.
40.
41.
42.
43.
44.
45.
46.
47.
48.
49.
50.